Mary B. Harris, PhD
Editor

School Experiences of Gay and Lesbian Youth: The Invisible Minority

School Experiences of Gay and Lesbian Youth: The Invisible Minority has been co-published simultaneously as *Journal of Gay & Lesbian Social Services*, Volume 7, Number 4 1997.

Pre-publication
REVIEWS,
COMMENTARIES,
EVALUATIONS . . .

"**T**his volume presents the diverse experiences and worlds of sexual-minority youths–in both tragic and inspiring terms. The contents of the chapters will be of value to practitioners, educators, researchers, policy analysts, and clinicians."

Ritch C. Savin-Williams, PhD
Professor of Developmental & Clinical Psychology,
Department of Human Development,
Cornell University
Author of ". . . and then I became gay":
Young Men's Stories *(1998) and (with K. M. Cohen)* The Lives of Lesbians, Gays, and Bisexuals: Children to Adults *(1996)*

"**F**inally! A book that presents some new views and issues regarding gay, lesbian, and bisexual youth. Not only does this collection present solid research about these youth and their views, it utilizes youth views that can be generalizable to others experiencing similar dilemmas around the country. Perhaps its most significant contribution is that it targets social institutions, specifically schools, for change.

This book is for all school personnel, advocates, and activists who believe each and every young person is worth our time, effort, and love. It gives specific ways in which each of us can break the silence, fear and isolation that gay youth experience within most school settings, and blazes a path toward long-term change. Use this collection in developing your school's action plan for being a welcoming and inclusive learning environment for ALL students!"

Jodi Brookins-Fisher, PhD, CHES
Assistant Professor,
Central Michigan University

"**S**chool *Experiences of Gay and Lesbian Youth* fills a gaping hole in the research literature on marginalized or minority students. The experiences of lesbian and gay young people in schools are described in a scholarly and accessible manner. This volume should be required reading for all teachers, teacher educators and others concerned about social justice in schools. The experiences described in this book highlight the urgency of addressing the pervasive heterosexism in schools, not only for gay and lesbian young people, but also for their heterosexual classmates. Harris's selection of articles in this anthology are clear and reasoned voices in the midst of the more typical overheated hysteria and posturing we are used to when the topic of gay and lesbian youth in schools is raised."

Pat Griffin, EdD
Associate Professor in Social Justice Education,
University of Massachussets, Amherst

"**S**chool *Experiences of Gay and Lesbian Youth: The Invisible Minority* is a call to action. Educators, researchers, politicians, advocates, and citizens of all ages have an individual and collective responsibility to undo heterosexism and homophobia in schools. Harris's book demonstrates that unless all members of our school communities are afforded the respect and opportunity to learn and thrive in a safe and empowering environment, the institution of schooling will fail.

The scholars in this book document how we are bankrupting the next generation through active silencing, institutional disenfranchisement and the creation of hostile school climates. The future of our society is being shaped in the hearts, heads and hands of young people in schools today. This includes lesbian, gay, bisexual, transgendered and questioning youth. The extent to which we can transform schooling so that gay and lesbian youth, teachers and families have a place at the table . . . schools can be a place of possibility for *all* people.

Richard A. Friend, PhD
Faculty, Human Sexuality Education,
University of Pennsylvania,
Graduate School of Education

The Harrington Park Press

School Experiences
of Gay and Lesbian Youth:
The Invisible Minority

School Experiences of Gay and Lesbian Youth: The Invisible Minority has been co-published simultaneously as *Journal of Gay & Lesbian Social Services*, Volume 7, Number 4 1997.

School Experiences
of Gay and Lesbian Youth:
The Invisible Minority

Mary B. Harris, PhD
Editor

School Experiences of Gay and Lesbian Youth: The Invisible Minority, edited by Mary B. Harris, was simultaneously issued by The Haworth Press, Inc., under the same title, as a special issue of the *Journal of Gay & Lesbian Social Services,* Volume 7, Number 4, 1997, James J. Kelly, Editor.

The Harrington Park Press
An Imprint of
The Haworth Press, Inc.
New York • London

1-56023-109-2

Published by

The Harrington Park Press, 10 Alice Street, Binghamton, NY 13904-1580 USA

The Harrington Park Press is an imprint of The Haworth Press, Inc., 10 Alice Street, Binghamton, NY 13904-1580 USA.

School Experiences of Gay and Lesbian Youth: The Invisible Minority has been co-published simultaneously as *Journal of Gay & Lesbian Social Services*, Volume 7, Number 4 1997.

The development, preparation, and publication of this work has been undertaken with great care. However, the publisher, employees, editors, and agents of The Haworth Press and all imprints of The Haworth Press, Inc., including The Haworth Medical Press and The Pharmaceutical Products Press, are not responsible for any errors contained herein or for consequences that may ensue from use of materials or information contained in this work. Opinions expressed by the author(s) are not necessarily those of The Haworth Press, Inc.

Cover design by Thomas J. Mayshock Jr.

Library of Congress Cataloging-in-Publication Data

School experiences of gay and lesbian youth : the invisble minority / Mary B. Harris, editor.
    p. cm.
    "Co-published simultaneously as Journal of gay & lesbian social services, volume 7, number 4, 1997"–T.p. verso.
    Includes bibliographical references and index.
    ISBN 0-7890-0376-7 (alk. paper). -- ISBN 1-56023-109-2 (pbk. : alk. paper)
    1. Gay students–United States. 2. Lesbian students–United States. 3. Homophobia–United States. I. Harris, Mary B. (Mary Bierman), 1943- .
LC2575.S36 1997
371.826'64–dc21
                  -41783
                  CIP

INDEXING & ABSTRACTING

Contributions to this publication are selectively indexed or abstracted in print, electronic, online, or CD-ROM version(s) of the reference tools and information services listed below. This list is current as of the copyright date of this publication. See the end of this section for additional notes.

- *AIDS Newsletter c/o CAB International/CAB ACCESS...* *available in print, diskettes updated weekly, and on INTERNET. Providing full bibliographic listings, author affiliation, augmented keyword searching,* CAB International, P.O. Box 100,Wallingford Oxon OX10 8DE, United Kingdom

- *Cambridge Scientific Abstracts, Risk Abstracts,* 7200 Wisconsin Avenue #601, Bethesda, MD 20814

- *caredata CD: the social and community care database,* National Institute for Social Work, 5 Tavistock Place, London WC1H 9SS, England

- *CNPIEC Reference Guide: Chinese National Directory of Foreign Periodicals,* P.O. Box 88, Beijing, People's Republic of China

- *Criminal Justice Abstracts,* Willow Tree Press, 15 Washington Street, 4th Floor, Newark, NJ 07102

- *Digest of Neurology and Psychiatry,* The Institute of Living, 400 Washington Street, Hartford, CT 06106

- *ERIC Clearinghouse on Urban Education (ERIC/CUE),* Teachers College, Columbia University, Box 40, New York, NY 10027

- *Family Studies Database (online and CD/ROM),* National Information Services Corporation, 306 East Baltimore Pike, 2nd Floor, Media, PA 19063

- *HOMODOK/"Relevant" Bibliographic Database,* Documentation Centre for Gay & Lesbian Studies, University of Amsterdam (selective printed abstracts in "Homologie" and bibliographic computer databases covering cultural, historical, social and political aspects of gay & lesbian topics), c/o HOMODOK-ILGA Archive, O. Z. Achterburgwal 185, NL-1012 DK, Amsterdam, The Netherlands

(continued)

- *IBZ International Bibliography of Periodical Literature,* Zeller Verlag GmbH & Co., P.O.B. 1949, d-49009 Osnabruck, Germany

- *Index to Periodical Articles Related to Law,* University of Texas, 727 East 26th Street, Austin, TX 78705

- *INTERNET ACCESS (& additional networks) Bulletin Board for Libraries ("BUBL"), coverage of information resources on INTERNET, JANET, and other networks.*
  - <URL:http://bubl.ac.uk/>
  - The new locations will be found under <URL:http://bubl.ac. uk/link/>.
  - Any existing BUBL users who have problems finding information on the new service should contact the BUBL help line by sending e-mail to <bubl@bubl.ac.uk>.
  The Andersonian Library, Curran Building, 101 St. James Road, Glasgow G4 0NS, Scotland

- *Mental Health Abstracts (online through DIALOG),* IFI/Plenum Data Company, 3202 Kirkwood Highway, Wilmington, DE 19808

- *Referativnyi Zhurnal (Abstracts Journal of the Institute of Scientific Information of the Republic of Russia),* The Institute of Scientific Information, Baltijskaja ul., 14, Moscow A-219, Republic of Russia

- *Social Work Abstracts,* National Association of Social Workers, 750 First Street NW, 8th Floor, Washington, DC 20002

- *Sociological Abstracts (SA),* Sociological Abstracts, Inc., P.O. Box 22206, San Diego, CA 92192-0206

- *Studies on Women Abstracts,* Carfax Publishing Company, P.O. Box 25, Abingdon, Oxon OX14 3UE, United Kingdom

- *Violence and Abuse Abstracts: A Review of Current Literature on Interpersonal Violence (VAA),* Sage Publications, Inc., 2455 Teller Road, Newbury Park, CA 91320

(continued)

SPECIAL BIBLIOGRAPHIC NOTES

related to special journal issues (separates)
and indexing/abstracting

- ❑ indexing/abstracting services in this list will also cover material in any "separate" that is co-published simultaneously with Haworth's special thematic journal issue or DocuSerial. Indexing/abstracting usually covers material at the article/chapter level.

- ❑ monographic co-editions are intended for either non-subscribers or libraries which intend to purchase a second copy for their circulating collections.

- ❑ monographic co-editions are reported to all jobbers/wholesalers/approval plans. The source journal is listed as the "series" to assist the prevention of duplicate purchasing in the same manner utilized for books-in-series.

- ❑ to facilitate user/access services all indexing/abstracting services are encouraged to utilize the co-indexing entry note indicated at the bottom of the first page of each article/chapter/contribution.

- ❑ this is intended to assist a library user of any reference tool (whether print, electronic, online, or CD-ROM) to locate the monographic version if the library has purchased this version but not a subscription to the source journal.

- ❑ individual articles/chapters in any Haworth publication are also available through the Haworth Document Delivery Service (HDDS).

CONTENTS

ABOUT THE EDITOR

Mary B. Harris, PhD, is Regents Professor in the College of Education at the University of New Mexico in Albuquerque. She has been Visiting Professor at the Ohio State University, the University of New South Wales, and the University of Georgia. Author of a number of articles about attitudes toward gays and lesbians, gay and lesbian parents, and gender role stereotypes, Dr. Harris received her bachelor's degree in psychology from Harvard University and her PhD in psychology from Stanford University.

FOREWORD

Schools:
The Neglected Site
of Queer Activists

Eric Rofes

Almost ten years ago, I published an essay in the *Harvard Educational Review* which examined issues surrounding the failure of schools to meet the educational, social, and cultural needs of lesbian and gay youth. "Opening Up the Classroom Closet" (Rofes, 1989) provided an analysis of the historic silences about

Eric Rofes, MA, teaches "Gay and Lesbian Issues in Schools" at UC Berkeley's Graduate School of Education. He is the author of eight books, most recently *Reviving the Tribe: Regenerating Gay Men's Sexuality and Culture in the Ongoing Epidemic* (The Haworth Press, Inc., 1996).

Address correspondence to Eric Rofes, University of California at Berkeley, 2775 Market Street #108, San Francisco, CA 94114. E-mail: erofes@uclink2.berkeley.edu

[Haworth co-indexing entry note]: "Schools: The Neglected Site of Queer Activists." Rofes, Eric. Co-published simultaneously in *Journal of Gay & Lesbian Social Services* (The Haworth Press, Inc.) Vol. 7, No. 4, 1997, pp. xv-xx; and: *School Experiences of Gay and Lesbian Youth: The Invisible Minority* (ed: Mary B. Harris) The Haworth Press, Inc., 1997, pp. xiii-xviii; and: *School Experiences of Gay and Lesbian Youth: The Invisible Minority* (ed: Mary B. Harris) The Harrington Park Press, an imprint of The Haworth Press, Inc., 1997, pp. xiii-xviii. Single or multiple copies of this article are available for a fee from The Haworth Document Delivery Service [1-800-342-9678, 9:00 a.m. - 5:00 p.m. (EST). E-mail address: getinfo@haworth.com].

homosexuality in the formal curriculum of most schools, and explored the failure of lesbian and gay male adults to forge change within systems of education in the United States. The essay presented two programs intended to provide support and educational options to lesbian, gay, bisexual, and transgender students in the public school systems of Los Angeles and New York City.

Over the past decade, this essay has been included in countless academic readers for courses in schools of education, social work, psychology, sociology, and public health. At times, I have wondered whether this paper is out-of-date. Certainly the programs discussed–New York's Harvey Milk School and Los Angeles' Project 10–have expanded and changed over the decade. With the great spotlight shined on gay issues throughout the 1990s, I expected to see significant changes in the experiences of queer youth in schools. If the nation's president discusses "gays in the military" on the evening news, and Ellen DeGeneres and her television sit-com counterpart come out of the closet, isn't it likely that queer discourse would seep into our nation's schools and create shifts in the social worlds of youth? If corporations offer employees domestic partner benefits and states approve gay rights bills, shouldn't youth cultures reflect similar progressive shifts?

The papers in this special collection make it abundantly clear that the school-based lives of lesbian, gay and bisexual youth continue to be fraught with silences, denials, dangers, and omissions. With a few notable exceptions, the heteronormativity of schools (Fine, 1993; Friend, 1993) remains intransigent, resisting reform as schools have long avoided pedagogical innovation (Tyack & Cuban, 1995). In the past decades no cities have opened schools paralleling the Harvey Milk School and few have made significant attempts to integrate Project 10-type counseling programs into the public schools. While new school reform initiatives such as charter schools are producing niche schools throughout the nation addressing the specific needs of populations long neglected in the public schools (deaf students, pregnant teens, school dropouts, Native American youth), gay organizers have yet to seize on reform initiatives to create appropriate schools for queer youth. The programmatic progress we've seen throughout the United States primarily has focused on the development of gay/straight alliances in high schools (Blumenfeld, 1995).

Those committed to creating welcoming schools for queer youth must reflect back on the decade and ponder why so little has changed. What lessons can we take away from these efforts which might inform our future work and deepen its effects on school climate, youth and faculty cultures, curriculum design and classroom pedagogical practices? How can the position of lesbians and gay men be shifting dramatically in certain spheres–the media, urban politics, cultural work–yet remain frozen in the 1950s in other spheres, including schools?

The expanding discourse on queer youth–including the essays in this volume–highlights the challenges we face as youth advocates, school teachers and administrators, and academic researchers. Studies of lesbian, gay, and bisexual youth in K-12 schools are primarily retrospective studies utilizing survey methods or life histories situated primarily outside of schools (Kola, 1994; Rogers, 1994; Sears, 1991; Zemsky, 1991). While studies of queer students at the college level are emerging (Malinowitz, 1995; Rhoads, 1994), and ethnographic research of teens involved in social programs for queer youth exist (Herdt & Boxer, 1993; Reed & Geddes, 1997), attempts to engage in long-term qualitative study of the production of sexual identities within middle schools or high schools face formidable barriers (O'Conor, 1995). Yet this is precisely the kind of research we need if we are to develop a deep understanding of the complex interplay between resistance, reproduction, and identity formation circulating between queer youth and the institution of the school, and research utilizing these methods has started to occur (see, for example, Mandel, 1996). What does agency actually look like for a queer seventh grader? What role does drama club play as a site of cultural resistance and identity production? What relationship do closeted and openly gay teachers actually have to the sexual identity construction of youth in their schools?

These are not idle questions. Some have argued that the increasing visibility of gay issues in the public sphere has increased–rather than decreased–the harassment and stigma directed towards queer youth in schools (Due, 1995). While gender non-conforming youth in the 1960s might be derided and rejected by their peers, a range of social identities were available to them (for example, boys could be nerds, wonks, or oddballs; girls could be tomboys, feminists or "studious types"). By the late 1980s, such youth often were immediately categorized as "lezzies," "fags," "queers," and "dykes." As knowledge of the existence of lesbian athletes and gay pop singers spreads throughout popular culture, it becomes increasingly difficult for youth constructing counter-hegemonic identities to find cover. Schools may fail to provide support services or initiate inclusive curricula, but this doesn't prevent the closet doors of some queer youth from being ripped open against their will.

Increasingly, personnel in schools throughout the United States find themselves forced to deal with queer youth. Not only have school administrators been found liable for failing to protect students from school-based anti-gay harassment and violence, but anecdotal evidence is mounting that queer youth are coming out in their classrooms at increasingly early ages, some as early as fifth or sixth grade. While a few years ago, efforts to protect lesbian, gay, and bisexual youth focused exclusively on high schools, these days, junior highs and middle schools–as well as some K-6 grammar schools–find themselves grappling, not only with sexual minority teachers or Heather's two mommies, but with self-identified queer youth.

Two states have engaged in visible efforts to make schools safe for students of all sexual and gender identities. Landmark efforts to initiate systemic changes which will benefit lesbian, gay, and bisexual youth in Massachusetts merit greater documentation and visibility. Efforts in the state of Washington to document hate violence against queer youth are also important. Yet, perhaps most interesting for activists and academics alike to explore might be why it has been impossible to replicate that state's Safe Schools Program of Massachusetts and the documentation project of Washington in any other state.

Elsewhere I have argued that until activists working towards lesbian and gay liberation make schools a primary site for their social justice activism, not only will queer youth continue to experience isolation, invisibility, and very difficult identity management choices, but the gay movement will continue to be marginalized among the plethora of social change forces operating at the end of the 20th century (Rofes, 1997). Almost universally, the major gay political organizations tackle institutions such as marriage and the military, but devote few resources to the schools, and then, only in a defensive response to Right-wing homophobic attacks. Youth activists, responding to the social and cultural worlds they inhabit, have taken the lead in demanding changes in schools. It's time for adults who consider themselves activists, organizers, researchers, and teachers to collectively forge a long-term, pro-active strategy for changing schools.

REFERENCES

Blumenfeld, W. (1995). "Gay/straight" alliances: Transforming pain to pride. In G. Unks (Ed.), *The gay teen* (pp. 211-224). New York: Routledge.

Due, L. (1995). *Joining the tribe: Growing up gay & lesbian in the '90s.* New York: Anchor Books.

Fine, M. (1993). Sexuality, schooling, and adolescent females: The missing discourse of desire. In L. Weis & M. Fine (Eds.), *Beyond silenced voices.* Albany: State University of New York Press.

Friend, R. (1993). Choices not closets: Heterosexism and homophobia in schools. In L. Weis & M. Fine (Eds.), *Beyond silenced voices.* Albany: State University of New York Press.

Herdt, G., & Boxer, A. (1993). *Children of horizons.* Boston: Beacon Press.

Kola. (1994). A burden of aloneness. In D. Epstein (Ed.), *Challenging lesbian and gay inequalities in education* (pp. 49-64). Buckingham, England: Open University Press.

Malinowitz, H. (1995). *Textual orientations: Lesbian and gay students and the making of discourse communities.* Portsmouth, NH: Heinemann.

Mandel, L.S. (1996, April). Constructing gender identity: Learning to be heterosexual in junior high school? Paper presented at the American Educational Research Association, New York.

O'Conor, A. (1995). Breaking the silence: Writing about gay, lesbian, and bisexual teenagers. In D. Unks (Ed.), *The gay teen* (pp. 13-16). New York: Routledge.

Reed, D., & Geddes, J. (1997, March). Gay youth at a social gathering: Play and identity development. Paper presented at the annual meeting of the American Educational Research Association, Chicago.

Rhoads, R. (1994). *Coming out in college: The struggle for a queer identity.* Westport, CT: Bergin & Garvey.

Rofes, E. (1989, November). Opening up the classroom closet: Responding to the educational needs of gay and lesbian youth. *Harvard Educational Review, 59*(4), 444-453.

Rofes, E. (1997, Spring). Gay issues, schools, and the right-wing backlash. *Rethinking Schools, 11* (3), 1, 4-6.

Rogers, M. (1994). Growing up lesbian: The role of the school. In D. Epstein (Ed.), *Challenging lesbian and gay inequalities in education* (pp. 31-48). Buckingham, England: Open University Press.

Sears, J. (1991). *Growing up gay in the South: Race, gender and journeys of the spirit.* Binghamton, NY: The Haworth Press, Inc.

Tyack, D., & Cuban, L. (1995). *Tinkering toward utopia: A century of public school reform.* Cambridge, MA: Harvard University Press.

Zemsky, B. (1991). Coming out against all odds: Resistance in the life of a young lesbian. In C. Gilligan, A. Rogers, & D. Tolman (Eds.), *Women, girls and psychotherapy: Reframing resistance.* New York: The Harrington Park Press.

PREFACE

Images of the Invisible Minority

Recently, I talked in a colleague's class about some research that Gail Bliss and I had conducted on teachers' views of students who have gay or lesbian parents. The course was called something like "Multicultural Issues in Education," and the students in the class were graduate students and teachers dedicated to valuing children from different cultural backgrounds and to encouraging students to develop as individuals. I expected some nods of recognition and some gasps of horror as I discussed what teachers had revealed to us in an anonymous survey. Yet from these well-intentioned teachers who chose to take a course on multicultural issues came comments like "but people don't *choose* their ethnicity [as they do their sexual orientation]," "If I were to mention homosexuality [in a class] I would be fired" and "Well, of course I tell children that they shouldn't say 'faggot', but I can't discuss what it means or why it's wrong." Many repeated their fears that if they were to speak up, if they were to even mention to the children in their classes that not

[Haworth co-indexing entry note]: "Images of the Invisible Minority." Harris, Mary B. Co-published simultaneously in *Journal of Gay & Lesbian Social Services* (The Haworth Press, Inc.) Vol. 7, No. 4, 1997, pp. xxi-xxiv; and: *School Experiences of Gay and Lesbian Youth: The Invisible Minority* (ed: Mary B. Harris) The Haworth Press, Inc., 1997, pp. xix-xxii; and: *School Experiences of Gay and Lesbian Youth: The Invisible Minority* (ed: Mary B. Harris) The Harrington Park Press, an imprint of The Haworth Press, Inc., 1997, pp. xix-xxii. Single or multiple copies of this article are available for a fee from The Haworth Document Delivery Service [1-800-342-9678, 9:00 a.m. - 5:00 p.m. (EST). E-mail address: getinfo@haworth.com].

xix

everyone is heterosexual, parents would be complaining and their credibility would be lost. As my colleague subsequently pointed out, these were the same comments that would have been made about civil rights 35 years ago. And as Fontaine indicates in her article, the legal system is beginning to consider the civil rights of gay and lesbian students just as it earlier considered the civil rights of ethnic minority students.

If well-meaning, well-educated teachers express such attitudes in the spring of 1997, then the information and ideas presented in this volume are desperately needed. Indeed many of the themes that appeared in the class discussion–overt harassment of homosexual students, refusal to discuss sexual orientation, fear of repercussions such as losing one's job–are also found in the manuscripts which follow. These are not local or idiosyncratic issues. The authors of the papers in this volume come from Florida, Illinois, Indiana, New Mexico, Pennsylvania, and Utah, and they report on gays and lesbians from all over the United States. Although the articles discuss different data and use different methodologies, it is clear that there is a lot of communality in their observations, concerns, and conclusions.

The intent of this volume was to discuss the lives of gay and lesbian youth in schools from a number of perspectives. The following papers show how this goal was realized. Morrow considers the process of career development in gay and lesbian youth. Jordan, Vaughan, and Woodworth report data from lesbian, gay, and bisexual students currently in high school on their experiences in school. Malinsky reports on email interviews with lesbian and bisexual females about what they endured in schools. Herr illustrates her discussion of how the school environment can lead students to drop out of school with a case study of an articulate lesbian adolescent. Rey and Gibson look at college students who reported incidents of homophobic and hostile behaviors, many of which had happened when they were in high school. Harris and Bliss survey gay and lesbian adults about their experiences in high school, which they had attended approximately five to fifty years previously. Finally, Fontaine discusses ways in which educators and schools have failed to respond to the needs of gay and lesbian students.

The methods used in the following manuscripts vary noticeably. Some papers (Fontaine, Morrow) rely on conceptual analyses of the research literature, supplemented by references to other data collected by the authors. Another paper (Herr) is a combination of conceptual paper and case study. Yet another (Malinsky) uses qualitative analysis of email communications. Three papers (Rey & Gibson; Harris & Bliss; Jordan et al.) use more formal questionnaires, combining quantitative and qualitative analyses.

In spite of the different content and methods, all of the articles are consistent in their conclusions: Schools and classrooms are unwelcoming and even hostile places for gay and lesbian students. Students and teachers may actively discriminate against gays and lesbians, or they may more subtly do so by their silence. Teachers, counselors, and administrators may feel personal prejudice about homosexuality; may prefer to avoid the issue altogether, sometimes out of ignorance; may be sympathetic but frightened of discussing the issue openly; or may be gay but afraid to disclose their sexual orientation. Few role models or adults who discuss gay issues in a positive way are available. Gay and lesbian students are faced with the problems of negotiating a hostile environment, in addition to the normal adolescent problems of finding an identity and a career (Herr, Morrow). As several of the papers indicate in their titles, gay and lesbian youth may be silent, invisible, and fearful. Alienation, depression, and even attempted suicide are not unusual outcomes of attempting to survive in an inhospitable and even malevolent environment.

The findings are not all bleak. Several of the articles report individual instances of positive experiences and support from other students and school personnel (Harris & Bliss, Jordan, Malinsky). Although most of the papers indicate that disclosing one's sexual orientation can sometimes be dangerous, there is also evidence that disclosure can be empowering and positive. All of the manuscripts provide helpful suggestions for ways in which schools can become places which welcome gay and lesbian students and therefore better serve the needs of all students. Moreover, not only the articles but also their reference lists constitute a rich source of information and ideas for social workers, teachers, counselors, and other school personnel who are struggling with ways to help gay and lesbian youth. The challenge is to use these resources to transform schools into places in which gay and lesbian youth can experience and express their struggles with identity and other issues as openly as other students, instead of remaining an invisible minority.

Mary B. Harris

Career Development
of Lesbian and Gay Youth:
Effects of Sexual Orientation,
Coming Out, and Homophobia

Susan L. Morrow

SUMMARY. Despite a rapidly growing literature on issues confronting lesbian and gay adolescents in today's society, little has been written about the effects of lesbian/gay identity development, the coming-out process, and homophobia on the career development of lesbian and gay youth. This article first examines normal adolescent career development. Then, it describes the factors that impinge on the identity and career development of lesbian and gay adolescents, most notably the process of coming out to self and dealing with the homophobia of others. Next, it theorizes about the impact of sexual identity development, coming out, and homophobia on lesbian and gay adolescent career exploration and choice. Finally, recommendations for school practice (teaching, guidance, and counseling) and policy are made. *[Article copies available for a fee from The Haworth Document Delivery Service: 1-800-342-9678. E-mail address: getinfo@haworth.com]*

Identity and career developmental theories notwithstanding, many lesbian and gay young people spend their adolescence tra-

Susan L. Morrow, PhD, is Assistant Professor, Department of Educational Psychology, 327 Milton Bennion Hall, University of Utah, Salt Lake City, UT 84112. E-mail: morrow@gse.utah.edu

[Haworth co-indexing entry note]: "Career Development of Lesbian and Gay Youth: Effects of Sexual Orientation, Coming Out, and Homophobia." Morrow, Susan L. Co-published simultaneously in *Journal of Gay & Lesbian Social Services* (The Haworth Press, Inc.) Vol. 7, No. 4, 1997, pp. 1-15; and: *School Experiences of Gay and Lesbian Youth: The Invisible Minority* (ed: Mary B. Harris) The Haworth Press, Inc., 1997, pp. 1-15; and: *School Experiences of Gay and Lesbian Youth: The Invisible Minority* (ed: Mary B. Harris) The Harrington Park Press, an imprint of The Haworth Press, Inc., 1997, pp. 1-15. Single or multiple copies of this article are available for a fee from The Haworth Document Delivery Service [1-800-342-9678, 9:00 a.m. - 5:00 p.m. (EST). E-mail address: getinfo@haworth.com].

versing the minefields of coming out and handling homophobia instead of traveling the merely rocky road of personal, sexual, and vocational identity development that characterizes adolescence for most young people. As Hetrick and Martin (1987) pointed out, "The primary developmental task for homosexually oriented adolescents is adjustment to a socially stigmatized role" (p. 25). In this article, I address the typical process of identity as well as vocational and career development for adolescents. Then, issues impinging on the identity development of lesbian and gay teens—most notably coming out to self and handling the homophobia of others—are described. Next, I theorize about the impact of lesbian/gay identity development, coming out, and homophobia on the career development of lesbian and gay youth. Finally, I make recommendations for teaching, guidance, and counseling practice and policy.

WHAT YOUNG PEOPLE **SHOULD** *BE DOING* *IN HIGH SCHOOL:* *IDENTITY AND CAREER DEVELOPMENT*

Adolescence is typically framed as a period characterized by a search for one's identity and developing intimacy with others (Erikson, 1968).

> The primary developmental task of adolescence is the achievement of identity, a sense of who one is, along with all this entails—values, beliefs, feelings, goals, skills, deficits, and sexuality, to name but a few elements of this sense of self. A secondary, derivative task is to learn to manage the social roles that accompany identity—to master, in short, the demands of one's particular place in society. (Bohan, 1996, p. 141)

Lesbian and gay adolescents face many of the same challenges that adolescents who are heterosexual deal with: the task of moving from childhood to adulthood, the transition from family to friends as reference group, finding themselves as sexual and romantic beings, and making decisions about work and career directions.

More closely related to adolescent career development are Marcia's (1966) stages of identity resolution, which expanded on Erikson's work on the Identity versus Role Confusion stage of development. Marcia found identity resolution to be based on two factors: (a) the presence or absence of a crisis related to vocation, religion, or political ideology, and (b) the degree of commitment an individual held for a particular choice. He identified four types of identity resolution: (a) Identity Diffusion, in which a crisis related to vocational choice is not reached, there is no consequent commitment to a choice, and the individual does not perceive this state as a problem; (b) Identity Foreclosure, in which there is also no crisis, with commitment being made largely as a result of the values of others; (c) Identity Moratorium, in which the individual is in crisis and struggling to make a commitment; and (d) Identity Achievement, in which the crisis has been experienced and a commitment made.

Career theories have traditionally ranged from trait-oriented to developmental and learning-theory approaches. Holland (1973, 1985) identified six types of individual preferences–realistic, investigative, artistic, social, enterprising, and conventional–that, if people were to be satisfied in their work, should fit reasonably well with the corresponding work environments. During adolescence, young people have the opportunity to increase their understanding of self as well as begin to understand what kinds of work environments might provide the "best fit." Super's (1957) developmental perspective identified the period of adolescence as a time of exploration, in which young people investigate career options, become aware of interests and abilities, and develop skills. Krumboltz's (1996) learning-theory approach stressed that "the goal of career counseling is to facilitate the learning of skills, interests, beliefs, values, work habits, and personal qualities that enable each client to create a satisfying life within a constantly changing work environment" (p. 61). He stressed the importance of career education and encouraged career specialists to view their work as an educational, not therapeutic, endeavor. The career-education process for adolescents would involve the infusion of career-related activities in school, school-to-work initiatives, study materials (including books, magazines, audio and video media), simulated environments, and cognitive interventions.

Lent, Brown, and Hackett (1994) proposed a model of social cognitive career development (SCCT) based on Bandura's (1986) sociocognitive theory. In SCCT, Lent et al. described the development of academic and career-related interests throughout the lifespan and the subsequent transformation of those interests into goals and actions. Of particular relevance here are the development of self-efficacy beliefs and outcome expectations. Self-efficacy beliefs, according to Bandura, are the perceptions of individuals of their abilities to carry out certain activities. Self-efficacy beliefs arise as a result of reinforced (by self or others) performance accomplishments. Outcome expectations related to those activities are based on direct or vicarious learning experiences. Lent et al. proposed that individuals develop interests for career-related activities for which they feel self-efficacious and expect positive outcomes. Although self-efficacy beliefs and outcome expectations are believed to form early in life, adolescence becomes a time in which those beliefs may be modified through various academic and career exploratory activities, as well as through the informal network of information that guides young people toward their ultimate vocations. Brown and Lent (1996) suggested a number of interventions based on SCCT, including identifying foreclosed options, analyzing barrier perceptions, and modifying self-efficacy beliefs.

WHAT LESBIAN AND GAY ADOLESCENTS ARE REALLY DOING: MANAGING MULTIPLE IDENTITIES AND OPPRESSIONS

In addition to developmental processes shared by most adolescents, lesbian and gay youth are also in search of identities relative to their sexual orientation. Bohan (1996) noted that this process is extremely complex, in that lesbian and gay young people may come to identify as such without having had same-sex sexual experiences (and, in fact, young women may form a lesbian identity based on affective, not sexual, feelings). Young adolescents may, in fact, be more aware of being "different" from their peers than of being lesbian or gay; and clarity about that difference may not emerge until the end of high school or even later. Many theoreticians and researchers have proposed lesbian and gay identity development models (e.g., Cass, 1979, 1984; Coleman, 1981/1982; Troiden, 1988). Typical stages include (a) a pre-coming out stage in which the individual is not yet aware of same-sex feelings but feels marginalized and different; (b) identity confusion, characterized by awareness of sexuality and internal conflict over identity, along with feelings of further alienation and isolation; (c) identity comparison or redefinition, including avoidance or repair attempts at eliminating or explaining away homosexual feelings and behaviors; (d) identity assumption or tolerance, in which there is self-identification without full self-acceptance and which constitutes the first step in actually coming out to self; (e) identity acceptance, characterized by exploration, experimentation, and interaction with other lesbian- and gay-identified people; (f) identity pride, in which the individual immerses her- or himself in the lesbian or gay community and separates from the heterosexual community; and (g) identity synthesis or commitment, which involves integrating one's sexual orientation with one's overall identity and seeing oneself in the context of a larger culture. Fassinger (1995) and McCarn and Fassinger (1996) noted that lesbian identity may develop differently from that of gay men because of such influences on women's development as gender-role socialization and the advent of feminism. They pointed out that lesbians frequently know very early that they will support themselves, developing a sense of independence that may not be as common among their heterosexual counterparts. The overlay of lesbian identity on top of heterosexual female socialization creates a complex set of experiences that further confound the identity development of lesbian girls, adolescents, and women.

Minority-identity development models, including those theorized about lesbian and gay people, arise from the need for individuals who are members of oppressed or marginalized groups to come to grips with their oppression and marginalization. For lesbian and gay adolescents, identity development demands that the young person deal both with the process of coming out (to self and potentially to others) and with handling overt and internalized homophobia. In schools, the site of the majority of adolescent social experiences, lesbian, gay, and bisexual youth may be receiving a substandard education because of discrimination and harassment, absence of role models, heterosexist bias in texts and teaching, and a number of other factors (Fisher, 1996). Teachers and counselors in schools are often reluctant to intervene or make changes because of their own concerns about job security, lack of administrative support, fear of censure by colleagues, ignorance about the importance of these interventions, or their own homophobia.

THE EFFECTS OF SEXUAL IDENTITY, COMING OUT, AND HOMOPHOBIA ON THE CAREER DEVELOPMENT OF YOUNG LESBIAN WOMEN AND GAY MEN

The challenges associated with being a lesbian or gay adolescent in a homophobic society cannot be underestimated. They run the gamut from isolation, alienation, and family problems to harassment, violence, and sexual abuse (Hetrick & Martin, 1987; Martin & Hetrick, 1988). Lesbian and gay youth are grossly overrepresented among youth suicides and attempted suicides (Elia, 1994). In schools, lesbian and gay adolescents report not being able to talk with school counselors about their orientation, negative statements made by teachers and peers about homosexuals, and peer harassment and violence (Savin-Williams, 1995; Telljohann & Price, 1993). As a result, lesbian and gay youth are prone to truancy and leaving school (Elia, 1994). Fassinger (1993) noted that in school systems, where discrimination may be at its worst, the needs of these students are often ignored or silenced. Although research and theory have increasingly come on board to address these important needs of lesbian and gay youth, little information exists as to the effects of lesbian or gay identity on the career development process.

Homophobia in the society at large, in families, and on secondary-school campuses has pragmatic implications for the career development of lesbian and gay adolescents. Because of the lack of acceptance of lesbian and gay youth by families and peers, as well as harassment and violence in homes and at school, these young people are overrepresented among school truants, dropouts, and runaway children (Durby, 1994). No longer at school, lesbian and gay adolescents may foreclose on education as well as on a financially secure future. These young people may fall into work that is meaningless or, worse, harmful, such as prostitution (Savin-Williams & Cohen, 1996). If they remain in school, peer harassment and violence lead to low self-esteem, a lack of safety, difficulty in concentrating, and even post-traumatic reactions.

The literature describing lesbian and gay career development has largely focused on adults; however, many of the findings can easily be extrapolated to adolescents. Morgan and Brown (1991) noted that minority-group models of career development stress the concept of opportunity structures—"each person's subjective perception of which occupational choices may be obtainable options" (p. 281). Gottfredson's (1981) theory of circumscription and compromise supports this construct, in which, by virtue of socioeconomic class and gender, individuals rule out particular occupations deemed by society as inaccessible or inappropriate to them. Lesbian and gay adolescents, receiving cultural messages that it is unacceptable for them to work with children or in the military, may find their opportunity structures circumscribed by virtue of their sexual orientation. Gottfredson, along with other theorists, has stressed the importance of environmental variables in the career development of women. Farmer (1985) identified the importance of background, personal, and environmental aspects of career development. Sexual orientation may be considered a background variable for lesbian women and gay men. Personal characteristics and values of lesbians—such as androgyny, equality, and independence—may further affect career choice (Morgan & Brown, 1991). Environmental variables such as homophobia, traditional gender roles, and protective legislation may strongly influence the evolving career directions of lesbian and gay adolescents. Astin (1985) also pointed out the importance of the interface between personal and social factors that contribute to work-related choices.

Research by Morrow and Campbell (1997; Campbell & Morrow, 1995, August) on the career development of lesbian, gay, and bisexual individuals supports Hetherington's (1991) contention that "during the early stages [of lesbian or gay identity development], a bottleneck effect may disallow career exploration. In the coming-out process, other parts of a person's life are often 'on hold.' Grades may fall, and students may be shifting their social activities and friends. During such stress-producing changes, career exploration may be difficult" (pp. 134-135). According to Morrow and Campbell, in adolescence young people may lack the internal and external resources to deal adequately with *both* the normal identity and career developmental tasks of adolescence *and* their sexual identity development accompanied by coming out and handling homophobia. Morrow and Campbell's preliminary findings indicated that during adolescence, their participants focused *either* on their sexual orientation identity–placing in moratorium (or even foreclosing on) their career development–*or* on their academic and career pursuits, delaying the coming-out process until later in life. Even this delaying tactic appeared to have negative effects, as participants reported that they had been unable to find a satisfying career direction until they had reached a commitment or integrative stage of their sexual identity. It is likely that, with inadequate support and internal resources, Marcia's crisis related to vocational choice is superseded by that of sexual-orientation identity.

Evans and D'Augelli (1996) pointed out the dearth of role models as a significant problem in the career development of lesbian and gay youth. By late adolescence, college students already identify stereotypic gay male (photographer, interior decorator, and nurse) and lesbian (auto mechanic, plumber, and truck driver) jobs (Botkin & Daly, 1987); and the fields of decorative arts, fashion design, fine arts, and entertainment are seen as most welcoming of gay men (Jones, 1978). In addition to adults who can help them test these stereotypes, adolescents in the midst of exploring their sexual orientation and coming out to self are in great need of role models to help them weigh the pros and cons of disclosure to others and identify occupations and geographical areas that will be lesbian/gay friendly (Evans & D'Augelli), as well as addressing partner and dual-career concerns. Students who face double discrimination (lesbian women, bisexual women and men, lesbians and gays of color, Jewish and working-class lesbians and gays, and lesbian/gay students with disabilities) are often even more bereft of role models due either to greater invisibility as women or bisexuals or to cultural constraints of many ethnic groups, working-class populations, or other groups.

Morrow, Gore, and Campbell (1996), applying SCCT (Lent et al., 1994) to the career development of lesbian women and gay men, suggested that both self-efficacy beliefs and outcome expectations may be affected by living in a homophobic society. Gender identity, along with self-efficacy beliefs about career-related activities, forms well ahead of sexual-orientation awareness. Isay (1989) and others have found that boys who later grow up to be gay have gender-nontraditional preferences and behaviors as children. Parents, however, discourage gender-incongruent behaviors in children (Unger & Crawford, 1992), particularly boys, thereby limiting opportunities for engagement in activities that might contribute to self-efficacy. Chung (1995) stressed the importance of sex-role socialization in the development of vocational skills, noting that "people are afforded much more opportunity and encouragement to develop skills that are considered appropriate for their gender than to develop nontraditional skills" (p. 183).

Perhaps more important, according to Morrow et al. (1996), is the relative salience of outcome expectations for lesbian and gay adolescents. During adolescence young people become more aware of environments surrounding various jobs and careers and gradually come to identify which fields may be lesbian/gay friendly or antagonistic. For example, an individual who may have been a peer tutor, teacher's aide, and Sunday-School teacher may be shocked by the realization that a favorite teacher either has been fired or is extremely closeted because of being lesbian or gay in the educational system. An emerging career goal may be abruptly abandoned because of perceived risk. This may be a critical point at which either career development or sexual identity is foreclosed or placed in moratorium, sometimes for many years.

EMPOWERING LESBIAN AND GAY YOUTH: RECOMMENDATIONS FOR PRACTICE AND POLICY

Croteau and Thiel (1993) noted the importance of integrating sexual orientation into career counseling. This is a particularly important concern in relation to lesbian and gay adolescents in light of what appears to be a tendency to attend to *either* sexual orientation identity *or* career development. This integration can be enhanced by providing a lesbian/gay-affirmative environment in the classroom or counseling office, "enhancing the development of a positive gay or lesbian identity in the context of career development work" (p. 176), and "recognizing and integrating the reality of anti-gay stigma" (p. 177). The following recommendations for practice and policy spring both from the literature and from the foregoing discussion. Morrow and Hawxhurst (1997) suggested that empowerment, to be effective, must be facilitated at three levels: the personal, interpersonal, and social/political.

Personal. Interventions at the personal level include those that take place on a one-to-one basis, often individually with a student. At the personal level, in terms of empowering lesbian and gay students toward successful career development, there are a number of interventions that both teachers and counselors may initiate. First, the classroom or office environment must be perceived by students to be lesbian/gay friendly. Many advocates display subtle (but noticeable by lesbian/gay students) symbols of support such as a small rainbow flag or brochures that provide information or resources for lesbian/gay students.

Guidance counselors and teachers should beware of adhering to traditional gendered categories for occupations, as many students— not only those who are lesbian and gay—may be limited by strict adherence to traditional gender roles. Teachers and counselors need to retrain themselves, if they are not already gay-aware, by asking, "How would I talk about this differently if I knew this student were lesbian or gay?" When a teacher or counselor can determine that a student is lesbian or gay, it is important to include that factor in career-oriented discussions with the student, in private if she or he is not open about sexual orientation.

As noted earlier in this article, Brown and Lent (1996) suggested a number of interventions based on SCCT, including identifying foreclosed options, analyzing barrier perceptions, and modifying self-efficacy beliefs. When, because of absence of support for developing interests and skills, a lesbian or gay adolescent has foreclosed options, the teacher or counselor can reopen the dialogue, questioning why, for example, after having excelled in athletics and led her basketball team to a championship, a young lesbian is not considering a career in athletics. If a gay young man has decided he can never enter the teaching profession, analyzing barrier perceptions may include helping him look beyond his current geographical community to consider moving to a gay-friendly metropolitan area where gay teachers are welcome. Finally, self-efficacy beliefs may be modified, for example, by arranging school-to-work opportunities in a field that it appears a lesbian or gay student has foreclosed in order to provide greater exposure as well as real and vicarious learning experiences and reinforcements on the job.

Interpersonal. Interventions at the interpersonal level involve activities that go beyond the teacher's or counselor's one-to-one relationship with the student and, in the case of career development, may include providing role models for lesbian/gay students, constructing a classroom climate to provide a lesbian/gay affirmative environment, and providing experiences in the total classroom or school context that support the development of all students. It is ideal if lesbian, gay, and bisexual teachers and counselors can be "out." These role models can make an essential difference in the career plans of students. In school and community environments that do not permit professionals to be open about their sexual orientation, there are still many ways in which these adults can affirm their lesbian, gay, and bisexual students. Often the existence of a trusting, respectful relationship where the adolescent can be herself or himself can provide support that may be lacking at home or in other environments. Career self-efficacy may be enhanced as a student is encouraged to explore new avenues of budding interest.

Freeman (1975) addressed the problem of the "null environment" for women, in which there is neither overt discrimination against women nor particular effort to emphasize women in professions. In such an environment, women perform more poorly than their male counterparts. An affirmative environment for girls, students of color, and lesbian/gay students is necessary to provide equal opportunity for all students. In the classroom, it is a small step for a motivated teacher to include lesbian, gay, and bisexual role models from history, literature, and the community to enhance the learning process of all students, not just those of a homosexual orientation. Particularly in the area of career interventions, these role models are essential. Openly lesbian or gay professionals can, where permitted in the school district, talk with students about the challenges and rewards of being "out" on the job. Either lesbian/gay professionals or others who are willing to talk about diversity issues of all kinds can help students reformulate outcome expectations regarding certain careers.

Open discussions in classrooms about job discrimination, harassment, and hostile climate related to gender, ethnicity, sexual orientation, and other variables will help to inoculate minority-group students as well as educate majority students about challenges and solutions in the workplace. Lesbian/gay-affirmative perspectives on vocational guidance should be framed in a total multicultural context that includes gender, race/ethnicity, class, and other relevant variables.

Sociopolitical. At a larger systemic level, policies need to be enacted that will create a supportive environment for all students. Administrators need to declare and enforce a zero-tolerance policy for sexual harassment and hostile climate. School boards must resist the conservative backlash that would endanger a portion of the student population under the guise of protecting family values. More specifically in relation to lesbian and gay adolescent career development, policymakers must replace antiquated regulations of the "don't ask, don't tell" variety with a diversity-affirmative program of general education and career education that includes lesbian and gay concerns, role models, and printed materials.

In part, the successful career development of lesbian and gay adolescents depends upon an overall environment of support for diversity, particularly sexual diversity. Unless there is a pervasive atmosphere of respect for all students, individual career interventions will not be successful. More specifically, however, those responsible for helping young people prepare to successfully enter the world of work must become aware of the costs to society when the talents of a large minority of people are wasted. Not every lesbian or gay student will become a Michelangelo or a Gertrude Stein. Few will become Olympic medalists such as Greg Louganis or tennis champions such as Martina Navratilova. But each has the potential to become all she or he is able to become, to plan for and choose work that is personally meaningful, thus contributing to a richer and more diverse society.

REFERENCES

Astin, H. S. (1985). The meaning of work in women's lives: A sociopsychological model of career choice and work behavior. *The Counseling Psychologist, 12*(4), 117-128.

Bandura, A. (1986). *Social foundations of thought and action: A social cognitive theory.* Englewood Cliffs, NJ: Prentice-Hall.

Bohan, J. S. (1996). *Psychology and sexual orientation: Coming to terms.* New York: Routledge.

Botkin, M., & Daly, J. (1987, March). *Occupational development of lesbians and gays.* Paper presented at the annual meeting of the American College Personnel Association, Chicago.

Brown, S. D., & Lent, R. W. (1996). A social cognitive framework for career choice counseling. *The Career Development Quarterly, 44,* 354-366.

Campbell, B., & Morrow, S. L. (1995, August). *Influences affecting career development of Lesbians, Gays, and Bisexuals.* Poster presented at the 1995 Annual Convention of the American Psychological Association, New York, NY.

Cass, V. (1979). Homosexual identity formation: A theoretical model. *Journal of Homosexuality, 4,* 219-235.

Cass, V. (1984). Homosexual identity formation: Testing a theoretical model. *The Journal of Sex Research, 20,* 143-167.

Chung, Y. B. (1995). Career decision making of lesbian, gay, and bisexual individuals. *The Career Development Quarterly, 44,* 178-189.

Coleman, E. (1981/1982). Developmental stages of the coming out process. *Journal of Homosexuality, 7,* 31-43.

Croteau, J. M., & Thiel, M. J. (1993). Integrating sexual orientation in counseling: Acting to end a form of the personal-career dichotomy. *The Career Development Quarterly, 42,* 174-179.

Durby, D. D. (1994). Gay, lesbian, and bisexual youth. In T. DeCrescenzo (Ed.), *Helping gay and lesbian youth: New policies, new programs, new practice* (pp. 1-37). New York: The Haworth Press, Inc.

Elia, J. P. (1994). Homophobia in the high school: A problem in need of a resolution. *Journal of Homosexuality, 77*(1), 177-185.

Erikson, E. H. (1968). *Identity: Youth and crisis.* New York: Norton.

Evans, N. J., & D'Augelli, A. R. (1996). Lesbians, Gay Men, and Bisexual people in college. In R. C. Savin-Williams & K. M. Cohen (Eds.), *The lives of lesbians, gays, and bisexuals: Children to adults* (pp. 201-226). Fort Worth: Harcourt Brace College Publishers.

Farmer, H. S. (1985). Model of career and achievement motivation for women and men. *Journal of Counseling Psychology, 32,* 363-390.

Fassinger, R. E. (1993). And gladly teach: Lesbian and gay issues in education. In L. Diamant (Ed.), *Homosexual issues in the workplace* (pp. 119-142). Washington, DC: Taylor & Francis.

Fassinger, R. E. (1995). From invisibility to integration: Lesbian identity in the workplace. *Career Development Quarterly, 44,* 148-177.

Fisher, J. B. (1996). *The effect of an educational program on teacher and school counselor knowledge, attitudes, and beliefs regarding homosexuality and gay youth.* Unpublished doctoral dissertation, University of Utah.

Freeman, J. (1975). How to discriminate against women without really trying. In J. Freeman (Ed.), *Women: A feminist perspective* (pp. 194-208). Palo Alto, CA: Mayfield.

Gottfredson, L. S. (1981). Circumscription and compromise: A developmental theory of occupational aspirations. *Journal of Counseling Psychology, 28,* 545-579.

Hetherington, C. (1991). Life planning and career counseling with gay and lesbian students. In N. J. Evans & V. A. Wall (Eds.), *Beyond tolerance: Gays, lesbians and bisexuals on campus* (pp. 131-145). Alexandria, VA: American College Personnel Association.

Hetrick, E. S., & Martin, A. D. (1987). Developmental issues and their resolution for gay and lesbian adolescents. *Journal of Homosexuality, 14,* 25-43.

Holland, J. L. (1973). *Making vocational choices: A theory of careers.* Englewood Cliffs, NJ: Prentice Hall.

Holland, J. L. (1985). *Making vocational choices: A theory of vocational personalities and work environments* (2nd ed.). Englewood Cliffs, NJ: Prentice-Hall.

Isay, R. A. (1989). *Being homosexual: Gay men and their development.* New York: Farrar-Straus-Giroux.

Jones, G. P. (1978). Counseling gay adolescents. *Counselor Education and Supervision, 18,* 144-152.

Krumboltz, J. D. (1996). A learning theory of career counseling. In M. L. Savickas & W. B. Walsh (Eds.), *Handbook of career counseling theory and practice* (pp. 55-80). Palo Alto, CA: Davies-Black.

Lent, R. W., Brown, S. D., & Hackett, G. (1994). Toward a unifying social cognitive theory of career and academic interest, choice, and performance. *Journal of Vocational Behavior, 45,* 79-122.

Marcia, J. E. (1966). Development and validation of ego-identity status. *Journal of Personality and Social Psychology, 3,* 551-559.

Martin, A. D., & Hetrick, E. S. (1988). The stigmatization of the gay and lesbian adolescent. *Journal of Homosexuality, 15,* 163-183.

Morgan, K. S., & Brown, L. S. (1991). Lesbian career development, work behavior, and vocational counseling. *The Counseling Psychologist, 19,* 273-291.

Morrow, S. L., & Campbell, B. W. (1997). *Career development of lesbian, gay, and bisexual women and men.* Manuscript in preparation.

Morrow, S. L., Gore, Jr., P. A., & Campbell, B. W. (1996). The application of a sociocognitive framework to the career development of lesbian women and gay men. *Journal of Vocational Behavior, 48,* 136-148.

Morrow, S. L., & Hawxhurst, S. L. (1997). [Feminist therapy: Integrating political analysis in counseling and psychotherapy.] Manuscript in preparation.

Savin-Williams, R. C. (1995). Lesbian, gay male, and bisexual adolescents. In A. R. D'Augelli & C. J. Patterson (Eds.), *Lesbian, gay, and bisexual identities over the lifespan: Psychological perspectives.* New York: Oxford University Press.

Savin-Williams, R. C., & Cohen, K. M. (1996). Psychosocial outcomes of verbal and physical abuse among lesbian, gay, and bisexual youths. In R. C. Savin-Williams & K. M. Cohen, *The lives of lesbians, gays, and bisexuals: Children to adults* (pp. 181-200). Fort Worth: Harcourt Brace College Publishers.

Super, D. E. (1957). *The psychology of careers.* New York: Harper & Row.

Telljohann, S. K., & Price, J. H. (1993). A qualitative examination of adolescent homosexuals' life experiences: Ramifications for secondary school personnel. *Journal of Homosexuality, 26,* 1993.

Troiden, R. (1988). Homosexual identity development. *Journal of Adolescent Health Care, 9,* 105-113.

Unger, R., & Crawford, M. (1992). *Women and gender: A feminist psychology.* New York: McGraw-Hill.

I Will Survive:
Lesbian, Gay, and Bisexual Youths' Experience of High School

Karen M. Jordan
Jill S. Vaughan
Katharine J. Woodworth

SUMMARY. Much has been written about gay, lesbian, and bisexual students' negative experience, such as harassment and hate crimes, in high school. This study was undertaken to further explore these issues, as well as to elucidate the positive coping skills, traits, and experiences of the students. Thirty-four current high school students completed a questionnaire containing both original items and previously-developed scales. The majority of the students (73.5%) reported receiving support regarding sexual orientation issues from someone at school, and 41.2% reported that information regarding gay, lesbian, and bisexual issues was available from school staff. However, 35.3% reported a previous suicide attempt, a figure consistent with previous literature. Additional positive and negative high school experiences, as well as their interrelationships, are discussed. *[Article copies available for a fee from The Haworth Document Delivery Service: 1-800-342-9678. E-mail address: getinfo@haworth.com]*

Karen M. Jordan is affiliated with the Department of Psychology, DePaul University, 2219 N. Kenmore, Chicago, IL 60614. E-mail: Kjordan@wppose. depaul.edu. Jill S. Vaughan is affiliated with Southwest Cook County Cooperative Association for Special Education, 6020 West 151st Street, Oak Forest, IL 60452. Katharine J. Woodworth is affiliated with Community Family Services, 1023 West Burlington, Western Springs, IL 60558.

[Haworth co-indexing entry note]: "I Will Survive: Lesbian, Gay, and Bisexual Youths' Experience of High School." Jordan, Karen M., Jill S. Vaughan, and Katharine J. Woodworth. Co-published simultaneously in *Journal of Gay & Lesbian Social Services* (The Haworth Press, Inc.) Vol. 7, No. 4, 1997, pp. 17-33; and: *School Experiences of Gay and Lesbian Youth: The Invisible Minority* (ed: Mary B. Harris) The Haworth Press, Inc., 1997, pp. 17-33; and: *School Experiences of Gay and Lesbian Youth: The Invisible Minority* (ed: Mary B. Harris) The Harrington Park Press, an imprint of The Haworth Press, Inc., 1997, pp. 17-33. Single or multiple copies of this article are available for a fee from The Haworth Document Delivery Service [1-800-342-9678, 9:00 a.m. - 5:00 p.m. (EST). E-mail address: getinfo@haworth.com].

17

Recent research has demonstrated that sexual orientation is established early in life (Savin-Williams, 1990; Troiden, 1988). Youth today may be willing to identify and proclaim their sexual orientation earlier than previous generations, in part due to the increasing visibility of gay, lesbian, and bisexual people in the larger culture (Anderson, 1994). Thus, there are many school-aged youth who are lesbian, gay, and bisexual (with estimates up to 10%; Gonsiorek, 1993), and many of these students will be visibly out in the school setting.

Schools, particularly secondary schools, are often environments filled with homophobia, heterosexism, and strict rules about gender conformity (Elia, 1994; O'Conor, 1994). This atmosphere may not be conducive to the learning or personal growth of gay, lesbian, and bisexual students that should be occurring at school. Schools often fail to meet the needs of lesbian, gay, and bisexual youth for a variety of reasons (Krivascka, Savin-Williams, & Slater, 1992). For example, they may fear repercussions, such as an angry parent or school board. Alternatively, there may be a basic lack of awareness or knowledge about the issues relating to gay, lesbian, and bisexual youth. Finally, the teachers and staff may be suffering from homophobia (an irrational, distorted view of homosexuality or gay, lesbian, and bisexual people; Gonsiorek, 1993) and heterosexism (the belief that heterosexuality is the only acceptable and the best way of living; Blumenfeld & Raymond, 1989). Institutionalized heterosexism (i.e., discrimination at a systems level, sanctioned by those in power) serves to keep sexual minority students invisible and may range from neglecting to acknowledge the existence of such students to overtly hostile acts such as violence, ridicule, or graffiti (Elia, 1994). As Whitlock (1988) states, "Homophobia is so pervasive that many people do not perceive the mistreatment of gay and lesbian youth as wrong" (p. 4).

Lesbian, gay, and bisexual adolescents may face stigmatization and a significant number of stressors in the school environment. These include ostracism, physical violence, and verbal harassment by peers and teachers. Male youth in particular may hold predominantly negative stereotypes regarding lesbians and gay men, as evidenced by one study that found that 89% of the male adolescents (ages 15 to 19) surveyed reported that they felt sex between two men was disgusting and only 12% felt they could befriend a gay person (Marsiglio, 1993). Derogatory remarks by fellow students may go unchallenged by teachers and administrators, whereas a parallel racist statement would prompt a reprimand (O'Conor, 1994). As Krivascka et al. (1992) state, "Because of their own prejudices, school and agency staff may allow or even encourage name-calling, discrimination, and violence against sexual minority youths or those suspected of being gay or lesbian" (p. 11). Moreover, teachers may also make inappropriate or negative comments regarding gay, lesbian, and bisexual individuals. This complacency and complicity by the adults in the school environment significantly contributes to the unsafe school environment.

Gay, lesbian, and bisexual teachers and staff may be reluctant to support sexual minority students. As O'Conor (1994) states, "Unlike minority teachers, who can serve as role models to minority youth, gay and lesbian teachers must hide their sexual identity and distance themselves from gay and lesbian youth" (p. 11). This is a result, in part, of teachers feeling that their jobs may be threatened if they either identify as gay or lesbian or form alliances with gay, lesbian, or bisexual students. In addition, the myth regarding the association of pedophilia and homosexuality may make teachers fearful of accusations of sexual abuse, or they may fear charges of attempting to recruit students to a homosexual lifestyle (Gonsiorek, 1993; Savin-Williams, 1989).

CONSEQUENCES OF HETEROSEXISM IN SCHOOLS

A positive and safe school climate is necessary for productive teaching and learning (Tirozzi & Uro, 1997). As the school climate is often neither positive nor safe for sexual minority students, there may be a decline in academic performance, school failure, school dropout, and a decrease in involvement in school and extracurricular activities (Durby, 1994; Eversole, 1993; Krivascka et al., 1992; Remafedi, 1987). For example, Remafedi (1987) found that 80% of his sample had deteriorating school performance, 40% were truant, 30% had dropped out of school, and 40% had lost a friend.

In addition, there has been much discussion about the greater risk of suicide attempts and successes among gay, lesbian, and bisexual adolescents (e.g., Gibson, 1989; Rotheram-Borus, Hunter, & Rosario, 1994). The underlying assumption of these researchers is that the stress of victimization, rejection, or living in secrecy contributes to a higher rate of suicide attempts in sexual minority youth. According to Gibson (1989), "The root of the problem of gay youth suicide is a society that discriminates against and stigmatizes the homosexual, while failing to recognize that a substantial number of its youth has a gay or lesbian orientation" (p. 110). However, the research on this issue is not comprehensive or conclusive. For example, several recent reports have found that victimization is not directly related to suicidal behavior (Hershberger & D'Augelli, 1995) and that suicide completion may not be higher in gay, lesbian, and bisexual teens (Shaffer, Fisher, Hicks, Parides, & Gould, 1995).

Another risk faced by sexual minority youth is that of being inappropriately labeled as seriously emotionally disturbed (SED) and targeted for special education services. Abuses of this system, such as an adolescent whose mother had her placed in a locked residential program against her will and with no clinical need for such treatment, have been documented (Abinati, 1994). It is often assumed by the school system that the special education professionals will be better able to cope with the issues of gay, lesbian, and bisexual students; however, they may also have inadequate training and not be able to meet the unique needs of these students. As a result of being labeled SED, the student may be placed in a self-contained behavioral disorders classroom, be sent to an alternative school, or be sent to a residential facility when the school system or the parent feels unable to cope with the student.

POSITIVE EXPERIENCES IN SCHOOLS

Researchers have focused almost entirely on the problems encountered by sexual minority youth in the school context (Savin-Williams, 1989). However, contrary to much of the published literature, school is not an entirely negative experience for all gay, lesbian, and bisexual students. One study found that about 25% of their sample felt comfortable talking about their sexual orientation with the school counselor and that most had a generally positive response from both teachers and counselors after disclosure (Telljohann & Price, 1993). Most lesbian and gay adolescents appear to be psychologically and socially healthy (Savin-Williams, in press; cited in Savin-Williams, 1989). One prominent researcher has proposed a paradigm shift from a predominantly negative view to focus on lesbian, gay, and bisexual youth as "gifted children" (Herek, 1993; cited in Kielwasser & Wolf, 1994), due to their ability to survive into adulthood by virtue of their powerful and creative resilience (Kielwasser & Wolf, 1994).

PURPOSE AND RATIONALE OF PRESENT STUDY

Because much of the available research focuses upon the experiences of gay male youth (most of whom are Caucasian) and is retrospective in nature, this study was undertaken to explore the experiences of gay, lesbian, and bisexual students currently in high school, with an emphasis on obtaining diversity in ethnicity and gender. In addition, because much of the previous literature focuses on the negative aspects of sexual minority youths' high school experiences, an attempt was made to elucidate the positive coping skills, traits, and experiences of the students. Negative experiences, such as harassment and hate crimes, were also explored to determine the extent of these problems in the school setting.

Many of the analyses planned were primarily descriptive and exploratory. However, the following hypotheses were proposed. First, it was hypothesized that disclosure of sexual orientation would be negatively related to anxiety and positively related to positive affectivity and self-esteem.

It was also hypothesized that negative feelings would be negatively correlated with positive affectivity and self-esteem. Similarly, it was hypothesized that negative feelings would be correlated with anxiety and the frequency of peer and teacher use of derogatory words. Finally, it was hypothesized that negative feelings and anxiety would be related to negative behaviors (e.g., suicide attempts, use of drugs or alcohol, running away, dropping out of school), whereas self-esteem, positive affectivity, and level of disclosure were predicted to be inversely related to these behaviors.

METHOD

Participants

Participants were gay, lesbian, and bisexual high school students from the Chicago metropolitan area. Efforts were made to generate a diverse sample. All participants who completed the questionnaire were entered into a drawing for fifty dollars as an incentive for completing the lengthy questionnaire. Confidentiality was strictly maintained. Respondents were instructed not to place their name or any identifying information on the questionnaires, and drawing entry forms were separate from the questionnaires. The entry forms were destroyed after the drawing was completed.

Procedure

A questionnaire developed for this study included items requesting demographic information, previously developed scales, and original questions. Qualitative questions regarding advice for adults, how the youth felt empowered, and incidents of harassment were also included. The questionnaires were distributed through various means. First, questionnaires were given to adult leaders of regional youth groups, both at schools and social service agencies, with a request to distribute them to their members. Second, questionnaires were given to teachers and school personnel known to the authors to be supportive of gay, lesbian, and bisexual students. Finally, the authors attended a teen club and asked high school students present to complete the questionnaire.

Measures

Sexual Orientation. Sexual orientation was assessed using two measures. First, a question directly asked what label regarding sexual orientation the youth preferred. The options included "lesbian," "gay," "bisexual," "queer," "heterosexual/straight," "do not use any term," and "other." Second, because the trichotomous categories of sexual orientation are viewed as an oversimplification of the construct of sexual orientation (Coleman, 1987), the Klein

Sexual Orientation Grid (KSOG; Klein, Sepekoff, & Wolf, 1985) was used to assess orientation. The Klein scale was selected for this study because it conceives of a person's sexual orientation as a dynamic multi-variable process. It examines several aspects of sexual orientation; the ones included in this study were three directly describing the sexual self (attraction, fantasy, behavior) and two that describe aspects of the self considered important to the composition of sexual orientation (emotional preference and social preference). Under the assumption that sexual orientation is fluid and changes over time, the characteristics are assessed in the past, present, and as an ideal. The KSOG required the participant to provide 15 ratings on a 7-point scale, with 7 representing "same sex only" and 1 representing "other sex only."

Disclosure of Sexual Orientation. Two measures were used to assess the degree of openness about sexual orientation. The first, adapted from an instrument by Bradford and Ryan (1987), is an overall measure of the percentage of persons in seven categories (family, gay/lesbian friends, straight friends, teachers, other school staff, other adults, other peers) to whom the individual had disclosed his or her sexual orientation. The second, based on Schachar and Gilbert's (1983) Disclosure Scale, was used to determine more precisely to whom the students have self-disclosed. Participants were asked to rate 31 people (with two additional "other" spaces) on a 5-point scale ranging from 1 (i.e., the student has not told this individual about her or his sexual orientation and thinks the individual does not suspect) to 5 (i.e., the student has told this individual about his or her sexual orientation on a detailed level).

Anxiety. Anxiety was assessed using the trait scale of the State-Trait Anxiety Inventory (Form Y; STAI; Spielberger, 1983). This 20-item scale consists of items given a weighted score of 1 (not at all) to 4 (very much so). A total score is obtained by summing the weighted scores for the 20 items.

Positive Affectivity. The Well-Being Scale of Tellegen's (1982) Multidimensional Personality questionnaire is a measure of positive affectivity (i.e., positive mood states, such as happiness and satisfaction). The scale consists of eleven items answered in a true-false format, and a total score is obtained by summing the responses.

Self-Esteem. The Rosenberg Self-Esteem Scale (RSE; Rosenberg, 1979) is a 10-item scale designed to measure the self-esteem of high school students. This one-dimensional scale requires participants to respond on a scale of 1 (i.e., strongly agree) to 4 (i.e., strongly disagree) for each of the ten items. This scale has been successfully used with students from a wide variety of ethnic backgrounds (Fischer & Corcoran, 1994).

RESULTS

Characteristics of the Sample

Thirty-seven completed questionnaires were received; however, three were eliminated from data analysis, as the respondents indicated that they were heterosexual. Thus, 34 adolescents, 14 (41.2%) female and 20 (58.8%) male, were included in the analyses. All were current high school students, with the exception of one individual who had recently dropped out of high school. The sample was ethnically diverse with 17 (50%) Caucasians, 12 (35%) Hispanic/Latinos, 2 (5.9%) Asian-Americans, 1 (2.9%) African-American, 1 (2.9%) Arab/Middle Easterner, and 1 (2.9%) multi-racial individual. Various religious backgrounds were represented as well, with 18 (52.9%) Catholics, 4 (11.8%) Protestants, 2 (5.9%) Jews, 1 (2.9%) Hindu, 1 (2.9%) Muslim, and 8 (23.5%) reporting no religious affiliation. All participants lived in the greater Chicago, Illinois area.

The ages of the students ranged from 15 to 19 years of age ($M =$ 17.3). Six (17.6%) students were in the 10th grade, six (17.6%) were in the 11th grade, and 22 (64.7%) were in the 12th grade. In general, participants were doing well in school, with the mean grade point average (GPA) being 3.11 on a 4.0 scale (range 2.0 to 4.0). Two (5.9%) students reported skipping a grade (kindergarten and grade 7), whereas four students reported repeating a grade (grades 1, 2, 3, and 5). In addition, seven (20.5%) reported receiving gifted education services, whereas three (8.8%) reported receiving services for learning disabilities. Twenty-seven (79.4%) students reported that their future plans included college.

Twenty-seven (79.4%) participants reported having a romantic relationship with someone of the same sex, with the average age of first relationship being 14.7 years (range 7 to 18). Twenty-eight (82.4%) reported having a sexual relationship with someone of the same sex, with the average age of first sexual relationship being 14.5 years (range 7 to 18 years). There was no significant difference between age of first sexual relationship for females ($M = 14.9$) and males ($M = 14.2$) or between age of first romantic relationship for the two genders (females, $M = 14.6$; males, $M = 14.7$). Although not significant, there was a trend for females to have a romantic relationship prior to a sexual relationship, whereas males tended to have a sexual relationship first. Fifteen participants (44.1%) were currently single, ten (29.4%) were currently casually dating someone of the same sex, two (5.9%) were casually dating both men and women, six (17.7%) were in serious or committed relationships with someone of the same sex, and one (2.9%) was in a serious relationship with someone of the other sex. Nineteen (55.9%) participants reported being currently sexually active, with all of them reporting practicing safer sex.

Fifteen participants (15, 44.1%) identified as gay, with seven (20.6%) identifying as lesbian, seven (20.6%) identifying as bisexual, two (5.9%) as queer, two (5.9%) preferring no term, and one (2.9%) as other ("gifted"). The mean age of first identification as gay was 12.7 ($M = 10.0$ for females; $M = 13.1$ for males), whereas first identification as lesbian was 12.4 and first identification as bisexual was 14.1 ($M = 15.1$ for females; $M = 13.3$ for males). On the KSOG, the mean past sexual orientation rating was 4.42, the mean present rating was 5.48, and the mean ideal rating was 5.33. There was no difference between males and females on past (4.75 and 3.99, respectively), present (5.74 and 5.14), or ideal (5.45 and 5.15) ratings of sexual orientation.

Positive Experiences and Behaviors

Most participants (70.5%) reported feeling positive about their sexual orientation ($M = 4.5$ on a 5-point Likert-type scale, with 5 representing "great"). Additionally, 85.0% reported that their first coming-out experience was positive. Students reported being out to gay, lesbian, and bisexual friends most frequently (with a mean of disclosing to 73.5% of gay, lesbian, or bisexual friends), followed by straight friends (55.0%), other peers (36.7%), teachers (26.9%), other adults (25.9%), family members (25.3%), and other school staff (23.4%).

Eleven students (32.4%) reported that a club or similar group was available at their school. These groups included both gay/straight alliances and politically oriented groups. All eleven students reported that faculty or staff members, such as teachers, social workers, or counselors, had assisted the students in establishing the groups. Twelve students (35.3%) reported bringing same-sex dates to school-sponsored events, such as prom, plays, sport events, and concerts. Presence of a gay, lesbian, and bisexual group on campus was correlated with increased discussion of sexual minority issues in classes ($r = .801$, $p < .05$). Similarly, both presence of information in the library and information in special events (e.g., assemblies) regarding sexual orientation were correlated with greater discussion of these issues in class ($r = .529$, $p < .05$, and $r = .999$, $p < .01$, respectively).

Fourteen students (41.2%) reported that information regarding sexual orientation was available from school staff. The most frequently cited staff members were counselors or social workers, followed by gay/lesbian teachers and sex education teachers. The majority of the students (73.5%) reported that at least one person in the school environment was supportive of their sexual orientation. Teachers (56%) were the most frequently cited supportive person, followed by friends (23.5%) and social workers/counselors (20.6%).

Thirteen students (38.2%) reported that gay, lesbian, and bisexual issues had been discussed in the classroom, in courses such as English, social studies, health, sociology, government, and sex education. In addition, five students indicated that sexual orientation had been addressed during special school events, such as assemblies, drama productions, and "tolerance week." Furthermore, 14.7% reported that books regarding homosexuality were available in the school library.

Fifteen students (44.1%) were involved in leadership positions in various organizations. Examples cited included positions in the National Honor Society, school newspaper, student government, sports teams, and academic teams.

Negative Experiences and Behaviors

On average, students reported hearing peers using words such as "faggot" or "dyke" in a derogatory way once per day, whereas they reported hearing teachers using similar words less than once per month. However, teachers were witnessed to correct or discipline a student for making a derogatory remark less than once per month.

In addition, negative emotional experiences were assessed, with the experiences being rated on a Likert-type scale where 1 represented "never" and 5 represented "always." The students reported feeling all the emotional experiences sometimes (threatened or afraid, $M = 2.5$; different or separate, $M = 3.0$; alienated, $M = 2.7$; alone, $M = 2.9$; and rejected, $M = 2.7$). Interestingly, the mean STAI score for the sample was 48.09 ($SD = 12.66$), which is significantly higher than the normative mean of 40.57 for high school students, $t = 11.94$, $p < .01$. The mean score on the positive affectivity scale for the current sample was 14.17 ($SD = 3.43$), which was significantly lower than the normative mean (19.0; normed on college students), $t = 14.82$, $p < .01$.

Slightly fewer than half (44.1%) of the students reported that at least one person in the school setting was not supportive of their sexual orientation. Of those, 53% reported that the people who were not supportive were teachers, administrators, or staff. Furthermore, 50.0% reported experiencing some type of harassment (verbal or physical) at school. Of those, 47% reported that the harassment resulted in a physical fight.

Several negative behaviors were assessed. The frequency of these behaviors is reported in Table 1.

Hypotheses

Contrary to the hypothesis, disclosure of sexual orientation was negatively related to self-esteem ($r = -.399$, $p < .05$). However, disclosure was not related to anxiety or positive affectivity. No significant relationship was found between disclosure of sexual orientation and how the students felt about being gay, lesbian or bisexual. Similarly, there was no relationship between the reaction

TABLE 1. Frequency of Negative Behaviors

Behavior	Frequency	Percent
Considered running away	18	52.9
Considered suicide	16	47.1
Used alcohol or drugs to escape unpleasant feelings	16	47.1
Experienced a decrease in grades or school performance	14	41.2
Attempted suicide	12	35.3
Ran away from home	10	29.4
Transferred schools	9	26.5
Considered transferring schools	8	23.5
Considered dropping out of school	6	17.6
Dropped out of school	6	17.6

of others (e.g., parents, friends, teachers) to the disclosure of the youths' sexual orientation and how they felt about it.

Negative feelings were not related to positive affectivity, self-esteem or anxiety, suggesting that these questions tap a unique dimension. Negative feelings were positively correlated with the frequency of peer ($r = .373$, $p < .05$) and teacher ($r = .358$, $p < .05$) use of derogatory words. Furthermore, higher levels of negative feelings were associated with a lack of discipline by teachers when peers used derogatory terms ($r = -.462$, $p < .05$). While disclosure was not related to frequency of exposure to derogatory remarks, it was correlated with an increased likelihood of being a victim of hate speech ($r = -.429, p < .05$).

Finally, it was hypothesized that negative feelings and anxiety would be related to negative behaviors (e.g., suicide attempts, use of drugs or alcohol, running away, dropping out of school), whereas self-esteem, positive affectivity, and level of disclosure were predicted to be inversely related to these behaviors. It was found that higher levels of negative feelings were correlated with suicide attempts ($r = .541, p < .01$) and suicidal ideation ($r = .487, p < .01$). Similarly, lower levels of positive affectivity were correlated with suicidal ideation ($r = .528, p < .05$). Higher levels of negative feelings were also correlated with running away from home ($r = .603, p < .05$) and deterioration in academic performance ($r = .587, p < .05$). Anxiety, disclosure, and self-esteem were not associated with the negative behaviors.

DISCUSSION

Most of the students surveyed had at least some positive experiences in the school setting. Many were able to find supportive staff and peers, excelled academically, or held leadership positions. When asked about the coming-out experience, twenty-three students reported that coming out had been an empowering experience for them. For example, one student wrote, "I am more in touch with myself and I have a better grasp on the fight against discrimination," while another wrote, "Coming out to some degree offered me freedom to express other aspects of myself than sexuality." Others wrote, "I have the courage to be myself and be proud," "once I came out I felt more secure," and "I have found great support in friends and the community."

However, despite these positive experiences a large number of the students continued to have negative experiences in the school setting. For example, many were victims of harassment or witnessed peers or teachers using defamatory language. Of most concern is the high rate of suicidal ideation and attempts, which is consistent with previous literature reporting that approximately 30% of gay, lesbian, and bisexual teens consider or attempt suicide (e.g., Gibson, 1989). However, other negative behaviors were found at a lower level than in previous research (e.g., 17.6% reported dropping out of school and 41.2% reported a deterioration in school performance versus 30% and 80%, respectively; Remafedi, 1987). However, these frequencies are higher than would be expected among the general high school population.

Of interest is the connection between derogatory language in the school setting and self-harmful behavior. Frequent witnessing of derogatory language by peers and teachers, coupled with a lack of disciplining of offending students by staff, was associated with an increase in negative feelings (e.g., aloneness, alienation, rejection). In turn, these negative feelings were associated with higher risk of suicidal ideation, suicide attempts, running away, and deterioration in academic performance. While it is a great leap to infer that negative hallway and classroom language leads to such destructive behaviors, it does bespeak the importance of the school atmosphere in promoting the academic and psychological health of all students.

The rationale for the negative correlation between self-esteem and disclosure of sexual orientation is unclear. However, it is possible that students who are more out receive greater harassment, as is evidenced by the correlation between disclosure and likelihood of being a victim of hate speech. This greater level of harassment may be damaging to the students' self-esteem. This finding is contrary to previous research that finds a positive correlation between self-esteem and disclosure (e.g., Jordan & Deluty, in press). It is possible that developmental issues, such as general adolescent identity development, may make this relationship a more complex one.

Suggestions for Adults Regarding Support of Sexual Minority Youth

Qualitative data were collected to examine youths' feelings and attitudes about gay, lesbian, and bisexual adults, as well as peers and heterosexual adults. Most responses indicated a desire for adults showing greater acceptance and tolerance of the youths' lifestyle and needs. In addition, the youth wanted lesbian, gay, and bisexual adults to be more visible and honest about their sexual orientation, although not necessarily to make contact with the youth themselves.

In the school context, a resounding theme was the desire to have schools be safe places for learning and self-expression, without the fear of harassment or violence. There was a repeated plea for adults to make and enforce rules against bias and harassment (e.g., "punish people for using words like fag," "create a safe place," "confront the problem of homophobia"). In addition, the students wanted greater visibility for gay, lesbian, and bisexual issues in their coursework, where relevant, as well as better education regarding sexual orientation for all students. The students felt that school-based groups or clubs for gay, lesbian, and bisexual students, with administrative support and assistance, were an important part of making the school environment amenable to sexual minority students. Finally, the lesbian, gay, and bisexual students also focused on changes they would like to see in their peers. The theme of acceptance again re-emerged (e.g., "accept differences," "stop hating, start understanding," "accept me for who I am").

Comments About the Study

Although the results reported above are based on a relatively small, non-random sample, it is noteworthy that this sample was obtained through various avenues, including schools, social service agencies, and a teen club. This is a departure from many previous reports (e.g., Hetrick & Martin, 1987) that base conclusions solely on samples obtained through social service agencies, whose population by definition is in need of some psychosocial services. Thus, it is felt that these results are more broadly generalizable to gay, lesbian, and bisexual youth in the school system.

Due to the number of comparisons made in the data analysis, there is a possibility of Type I errors (i.e., a false positive or significant outcome resulting from chance). However, all but a few of the comparisons made were planned and specified in the hypotheses. In addition, the small sample size increases the probability of a Type II error (i.e., a false negative result). Thus, these results should be interpreted with care, and additional research should be conducted to further investigate the validity of these results.

CONCLUSIONS

One important lesson to be learned from this study is that positive things are occurring in high schools for lesbian, gay, and bisexual students. The truly bleak picture painted by many may not apply to all sexual minority high school students. However, it is important not to minimize the detrimental effects of discrimination and harassment on the students' academic performance and social growth. What school professionals must concentrate on is understanding, building, and enhancing factors (e.g., educational efforts; gay, lesbian, and bisexual clubs) that improve the school environment, and thus the quality of life for these students.

REFERENCES

Abinati, A. (1994). Legal challenges facing gay and lesbian youth. *Journal of Gay & Lesbian Social Services, 1*(3/4), 149-169.

Anderson, D. A. (1994). Lesbian and gay adolescents: Social and developmental considerations. *The High School Journal, 77*, 13-19.

Blumenfeld, W. J., & Raymond, D. (1989). *Looking at gay and lesbian life.* Boston: Beacon Press.

Bradford, J., & Ryan, C. (1987). *National lesbian health care survey.* Blacksburg, VA: National Lesbian and Gay Health Foundation.

Coleman, E. (1987). Assessment of sexual orientation. *Journal of Homosexuality, 14*(1/2), 9-24.

Durby, D. D. (1994). Gay, lesbian, and bisexual youth. *Journal of Gay & Lesbian Social Services, 1*(3/4), 1-37.

Elia, J. P. (1994). Homophobia in the high school: A problem in need of a resolution. *The High School Journal, 77*, 177-185.

Eversole, T. (1993). Lesbian, gay and bisexual youth in school. *NASP Communiqué, 22*(1), 7-10.

Fischer, J., & Corcoran, K. (1994). *Measures for clinical practice: A sourcebook: Vol. 1: Couples, families, and children* (2nd ed.). New York: The Free Press.

Gibson, P. (1989). Gay male and lesbian youth suicide. In the U.S. Department of Health and Human Services, *Report of the secretary's task force on youth suicide, Volume 3: Prevention and interventions in youth suicide* (pp. 110-142). Rockville, MD: U.S. Department of Health and Human Services.

Gonsiorek, J. C. (1993). Mental health issues of gay and lesbian adolescents. In L. D. Garnets & D. C. Kimmel (Eds.), *Psychological perspectives on lesbian and gay male experiences* (pp. 469-485). New York: Columbia University Press.

Hershberger, S. L., & D'Augelli, A. R. (1995). The impact of victimization on the mental health and suicidality of lesbian, gay, and bisexual youth. *Developmental Psychology, 31*, 65-74.

Hetrick, E. S., & Martin, A. D. (1987). Developmental issues and their resolution for gay and lesbian adolescents. *Journal of Homosexuality, 14*, 25-44.

Jordan, K. M., & Deluty, R. H. (In press). Coming out, self-esteem, positive affectivity, and anxiety in lesbian women. *Journal of Homosexuality.*

Kielwasser, A. P., & Wolf, M. A. (1994). Silence, difference, and annihilation: Understanding the impact of mediated heterosexism on high school students. *The High School Journal, 77*, 58-79.

Klein, F., Sepekoff, B., & Wolf, T. J. (1985). Sexual orientation: A multi-variable dynamic process. *Journal of Homosexuality, 11*(1/2), 35-49.

Krivascka, J. J., Savin-Williams, R. C., & Slater, B. R. (1992). Background paper for the resolution on lesbian, gay, and bisexual youths in schools, The American Psychological Association Council of Representatives Agenda, February 26-28, 1993, 454-489. (Available from the American Psychological Association, 750 First Street, NE, Washington, DC 20002).

Marsiglio, W. (1993). Attitudes toward homosexual activity and gays as friends: A national survey of 15- to 19-year-old males. *The Journal of Sex Research, 30*, 12-17.

O'Conor, A. (1994). Who gets called queer in school? Lesbian, gay and bisexual teenagers, homophobia, and high school. *The High School Journal, 77*, 7-12.

Remafedi, G. J. (1987). Adolescent homosexuality: Psychosocial and medical implications. *Pediatrics, 79*, 331-337.

Rosenberg, M. (1979). *Conceiving the self.* New York: Basic Books.

Rotheram-Borus, M. J., Hunter, J., & Rosario, M. (1994). Suicidal behavior and gay-related stress among gay and bisexual male adolescents. *Journal of Adolescent Research, 9*, 498-508.

Savin-Williams, R. C. (1989). Gay and lesbian adolescents. *Marriage & Family Review, 14*(3/4), 197-216.

Savin-Williams, R. C. (1990). *Gay and lesbian youth: Expressions of identity.* Washington, DC: Hemisphere.

Schachar, S. A., & Gilbert, L. A. (1983). Working lesbians: Role conflicts and coping strategies. *Psychology of Women Quarterly, 7*, 244-256.

Shaffer, D., Fisher, P., Hicks, R. H., Parides, M., & Gould, M. (1995). Sexual orientation in adolescents who commit suicide. *Suicide and Life-Threatening Behavior, 25* (Suppl), 64-71.

Spielberger, C. D. (1983). *Manual for the state-trait anxiety inventory.* (Rev. ed.) Palo Alto, CA: Consulting Psychologists Press.

Tellegen, A. (1982). *Brief manual for the Differential Personality Scale (Multidimensional Personality Questionnaire).*

Telljohann, S. K., & Price, J. H. (1993). A qualitative examination of adolescent homosexuals' life experiences: Ramifications for secondary school personnel. *Journal of Homosexuality, 26*(1), 41-56.

Tirozzi, G. N., & Uro, G. (1997). Education reform in the United States: National policy in support of local efforts for school improvement. *American Psychologist, 52*, 241-255.

Troiden, R. R. (1988). *Gay and lesbian identity: A sociological study.* Dix Hills, NY: General Hall.

Whitlock, K. (1988). *Bridges of respect: Creating support for lesbian and gay youth.* Philadelphia, PA: Americans Friends Service Committee.

Learning to Be Invisible: Female Sexual Minority Students in America's Public High Schools

Kathleen P. Malinsky

SUMMARY. This study is based on E-mail interviews with 27 self-identified lesbian and bisexual female high school students. The interviews were conducted in an informal style over a period of several months, permitting the participants an opportunity to respond to a series of questions, as well as voice any other concerns relevant to their school experiences. This process involved three distinct objectives: (a) to define the forms of homophobia and heterosexism in the high school environment, (b) to explore ways in which homophobia and heterosexism have impacted the participants, and (c) to propose ways to combat heterosexism and homophobia in high schools. This paper gives voice to these young lesbian and female bisexual students so that readers may develop a better understanding of the realities of their experiences in school. *[Article copies available for a fee from The Haworth Document Delivery Service: 1-800-342-9678. E-mail address: getinfo@haworth.com]*

Homophobia and heterosexism in the public school system have all but silenced any discussion regarding sexual minority students

Kathleen P. Malinsky, EdD, is Assistant Professor, The University of Sarasota, 117C Pompano Drive Southeast, St. Petersburg, FL 33705. E-mail: KAT56@aol.com

[Haworth co-indexing entry note]: "Learning to Be Invisible: Female Sexual Minority Students in America's Public High Schools." Malinsky, Kathleen P. Co-published simultaneously in *Journal of Gay & Lesbian Social Services* (The Haworth Press, Inc.) Vol. 7, No. 4, 1997, pp. 35-50; and: *School Experiences of Gay and Lesbian Youth: The Invisible Minority* (ed: Mary B. Harris) The Haworth Press, Inc., 1997, pp. 35-50; and: *School Experiences of Gay and Lesbian Youth: The Invisible Minority* (ed: Mary B. Harris) The Harrington Park Press, an imprint of The Haworth Press, Inc., 1997, pp. 35-50. Single or multiple copies of this article are available for a fee from The Haworth Document Delivery Service [1-800-342-9678, 9:00 a.m. - 5:00 p.m. (EST). E-mail address: getinfo@haworth.com].

35

(O'Conor, 1993-94; Reed, 1992; Sears, 1992; Unks, 1993-94). This research exposes the voices of lesbian and female bisexual high school students so that educators may develop a better understanding of the consequences of homophobia and heterosexism. Perhaps this understanding will lead to increased empathy for sexual minority youth and open the doors for a widespread examination of the silence, fear, and isolation that continue to harm sexual minority students.

The purpose of this study was to explore the problems that lesbian and female bisexual students face in the public high school setting. The primary research goal was to find out how young lesbians and female bisexuals feel about their experiences in America's public high schools.

This process in turn involved three distinct objectives. The first was to define the various forms of homophobia and heterosexism in the high school environment, as reported by the research participants. The second was to explore the ways in which heterosexism and homophobia have impacted the participants. The third was to propose ways to combat heterosexism and homophobia in high schools, thereby making them more gay friendly.

Although sexual minority youth of both sexes suffer from the homophobia and heterosexism expressed in schools, I chose to limit my study to lesbians and female bisexuals, because the bulk of research on sexual minority youth has either excluded or under-represented females. Research using exclusively or primarily male subjects abounds (Kissen, 1991; Mercier & Berger, 1989; Proctor & Groze, 1994; Reed, 1992; Roesler & Deisher, 1972; Remafadi, 1987; Remafedi, Farrow, & Deisher, 1991; Savin-Williams, 1990), while research on lesbians and bisexual females is limited. Only two studies dealing exclusively with lesbian high school age students exist and these were completed in England (Rodgers, 1994) and Canada (Schneider, 1989).

As Marigold Rodgers (1994) says, "Young lesbians are subject to triple invisibility: as children, they are invisible in the adult world; as women, they are invisible in a male-dominated world; and as lesbians they are invisible in a gay world" (p. 35). In recognition of the under-representation of the female sexual minority experience in current research, I limited my study to the experiences of young lesbians and female bisexuals.

METHOD

Participants

To reach the difficult-to-find population of lesbians and bisexual females under the age of twenty-five, I posted notices on various electronic bulletin boards catering to young lesbians. This required the participants to have access to an online service. Some of the participants had access through the university they attended while those of high school age had access to a computer and modem at home. Those who responded to my initial inquiry agreed to take part in E-mail interviews on the Internet.

The respondents were 22 self-identified lesbians and 5 self-identified bisexual females, ages 15 to 21. Four of the women identified themselves as minorities. These included one Chinese-American, one Pacific Islander, one Latina and one Vietnamese-American. The others were Caucasian. They came from a variety of religious backgrounds: Catholic, Jewish, Baptist, Presbyterian, Lutheran, Methodist, Quaker, Episcopalian, and Buddhist. All were either attending high school or had graduated and gone on to college. They were from middle to upper-middle class homes in rural, suburban, and urban communities. The participants reported on their high school experiences in twenty states within the continental United States. All the major geographical regions of the U.S. were represented.

Design and Procedure

I corresponded with the participants over a period of several months, and the informal style of our interactions permitted them to respond to prepared questions, as well as voice any other concerns relevant to the topic of investigation. Though the responses varied in length, all were detailed and involved a great deal of self-disclosure. Two factors may have influenced the participants' willingness to disclose the personal information which they shared. One is the cloak of anonymity which E-mail interviewing permits. The other is the fact that they were sharing this information with a lesbian educator who had expressed an interest in their experiences. To protect the identities of these young women, I use only their first initial and where they attend/attended high school to identify them in this report.

I used eighteen prepared interview questions based on the issues derived from reports of sexual minority youth (Governor's Commission on Gay and Lesbian Youth, 1993; Heron, 1994; McManus et al., 1991; Unks, 1993-94). The questions covered such topics as discrimination, overall school performance, information provided about sexual diversity, the existence of positive role models, access to counseling, and opportunities for social interaction.

This study is grounded in the lived experience of the participants. Though these participants are not necessarily representative, they speak for and about themselves. Through their words we come to a better understanding of what it means to be a female sexual minority student attending a public high school in the United States.

RESULTS AND DISCUSSION

The Forms of Homophobia and Heterosexism in Schools

Overt homophobia takes the form of verbal and physical abuse of sexual minority youth or those who are perceived as being sexual minorities. This harassment is expressed in the form of name-calling, queer jokes, AIDS jokes, snide remarks, gay bashings and other hate crimes (Governor's Commission on Gay and Lesbian Youth, 1993; Heron, 1994; McManus et al., 1991; Uribe, 1991).

Harassment of Sexual Minority Youth in School. Sexual minority youth learn from direct exposure to taunts, ostracism and fights that the high school environment is definitely anti-homosexual (Goffman, 1963; Hunter and Schaecher, 1987; Martin, 1982; O'Conor, 1995). In our public schools these youth must contend with an oppressive social environment that includes homophobia and violence against them. As two participants reported: "The students openly mocked people who seemed, in their opinion, to be gay. They made jokes and were generally cruel" (S., 19, Madison Co., Indiana). "Nothing said aloud was positive" (K., 19, Batesville, Indiana).

Many sexual minority youth learn the bitter lessons of homophobia through verbal and physical abuse. Only two participants reported no first hand knowledge of harassment. The others had all experienced some form of abuse in school. They reported:

> . . . harassment happened a lot at my hs [high school] . . . my best friend who was also a lesbian . . . had a very out gf [girlfriend] . . . and she was harassed all the time . . . a gun was even pulled on her. (D., 17, Pasadena, Texas)

> My Junior year, I started dating a friend of mine. . . . People would pass me in the halls and make derogatory statements. Teachers would make comments behind my back. The librarian told me that I was going to get what I deserved. Once or twice I was followed home from school, and once, I had someone throw a brick through my car window. Needless to say, my girlfriend and I were the topic of discussion for sometime. (L., 19, Homewood, Alabama)

> I experienced harassment by my classmates on a daily basis because of my presumed homosexuality. Thankfully, they only went as far as rumors and name-calling, but no violence. (K., 19, Batesville, Indiana)

Sometimes the abuse was directed at those associated with young lesbians/bisexuals:

> I myself have not encountered direct harassment because I am gay. I am largely out to my high school, but people are too afraid to air their grievances to my face. My friends, however, do get harassed. I have a friend who was stopped on many occasions at school to be verbally abused for being 'gay,' even though she is straight. They don't like it that she's friends with me, nor do they like her openly liberal stance on most issues. (F., 17, Orange County, California)

Institutional heterosexism is apparent in many forms. These include the lack of information on sexual diversity, the absence of positive role models and the failure on the part of the schools to provide counseling for these youth.

Lack of Information on Sexual Diversity. Struggling sexual minority youth can be helped by opening up the discussion of gay issues in our schools. Unfortunately, silence is what all but five participants reported. In response to the question, "Were lesbianism or homosexuality discussed in school?", only three participants reported any formal discussion of homosexuality unrelated to AIDS.

> The only positive mention in my classes (the negative ones were from peers, not teachers) came from my senior Psychology teacher, who stated, as I recall, that homosexuality was normal and healthy and that anyone who had questions or concerns about being gay or friends being gay could come talk to him. (L., 22, San Mateo County, California)

Many other participants remarked on the lack of information provided in their schools, "Even in sex-ed classes, there was no mention of any alternative to heterosexuality" (G., 21, Broward, Florida). Other participants shared:

> I would say that the most important thing to do is discuss the subject in class if at all possible; one thing that drove me nuts and still does is the complete lack of representation gays and lesbians have in the curriculum or even in general discussions. I think the sheer fact of omission of the subject leaves the implication that the subject is so evil that you can't even talk about it. Not quite a very encouraging environment. . . . (S., 19, Tulsa, Oklahoma)

> I don't remember any formal discussion of homosexuality in school. In fact, it's really surprising to me that we didn't discuss it. My required eleventh grade health class, come to think of it, covered everything but that. We did condoms, sex, teen pregnancy, suicide, eating disorders, every kind of cancer–you name it, we did it. But nothing on homosexuality. (D., 17, Monroe County, New York)

The silencing of information extended to written material as well. When asked if books or articles dealing with homosexuality were available at their school, seventeen of the responses were negative. Five reported limited resources and five found some information in the library. The participants reported:

> . . . there was NO material on gay issues in my town. And I looked for it, because although I wasn't really fully aware of my sexuality I was forever doing projects on AIDS, and les-bi-gay issues (to my teachers' dismay and disappointment). (R., 19, Fairfield County, Connecticut)

> I don't know if books pertaining to the issue of homosexuality were available in my school. I knew not to look for such things, because if you read about homosexuality, you were assumed to be a homosexual. (K., 19, Batesville, Indiana)

When the participants were asked to "describe the general attitude toward homosexuality at your high school" their descriptions were overwhelmingly negative: "The faculty made no mention and their silence was damning" (S., 19, Madison County, Indiana).

> The general attitude toward homosexuality: 'Homosexuals are sinners. AIDS is their punishment from God. They all deserve to die.' My classmates and government teacher made this very clear in class when they made these exact statements. All those who would scream out terms such as 'lesbo' at me in the hall and would tell me that I deserved to go to hell verified my initial impression. (K., 19, Batesville, Indiana)

> The general attitude towards gays at my high school swings from general intolerance to denying there is an issue to be dealt with at all. . . . Gay kids are not provided for, and are pretty much ignored. They don't care whether we live or die. I know that might sound like an exaggeration, but they really don't care. (F., 17, Orange County, California)

The Absence of Positive Role Models. Many sexual minority youth have spoken up about their need for positive adult role models in schools (Heron, 1994; Kissen, 1991; Martin, 1982; Uribe & Harbeck, 1992). The researchers who have studied homosexual identity formation describe a stage of development in which young people compare how they self-identify with their perceptions of being gay (Cass, 1984; Coleman, E., 1988; Herdt, 1989; Troiden, 1988). Because positive role models are not readily accessible to sexual minority youth, their perception of homosexuality is often negative (Kaplan & Saperstein, 1985). One participant describes her perceptions as she identified "as at least a bisexual person for the first time":

> How I felt was slightly relieved, but mostly scared out of my mind. I still thought of homosexuals as 'those people,' not as myself, and I still thought it was wrong. That began a very long struggle that I'm still going through. (S., 19, Tulsa, Oklahoma)

The presence of visible lesbian, gay and bisexual staff members is essential in providing support for sexual minority youth (Governor's Commission on Gay and Lesbian Youth, 1993; Kissen, 1991). Gay teenagers long for adult lesbian and gay role models and urge gay, lesbian, and bisexual teachers to come out to their students (Kissen, 1991). In this study, these pleas were made: "If you're gay and a teacher, be out and supportive to the students. I know this would be hard, but these students need positive role models" (M., 18, Whitfield County, Georgia).

> If you're queer, come out of the school coat closet. We need to see you! If you're straight, step back; realize that you live as a het [heterosexual] in a het [heterosexual] world and that you don't know what we live with; then open your heart and let down your barriers; step into our shoes; feel our shame, bewilderment, hurt, anger, self-realization, pride; help us. (H., 17, Santa Clara County, California)

> Well, adults have to understand that they are VERY important to us. More than they think. I've never really met a gay adult and I am quite in awe of them. Adults shouldn't be afraid to say that gay-bashing is really rude and inconsiderate, just like

racist jokes are rude. I never understood why it wasn't okay to make fun of a black kid but it was alright to harass a gay one. Educators are too often cowed by the parents so they won't say anything. I get angry sometimes. I know they have their jobs to look out for but I nearly DIED trying to get at least one of them to listen. A lot of us are truly thankful that we made it out of high school alive, because it was hell on earth for us. It doesn't have to be that way. (F., 17, Orange County, California)

Failure to Provide Counseling. Sexual minority youth have also expressed the need for the support of their counselors (Kissen, 1991). Failure to provide counseling or referrals for this population at risk is an act of negligence (Benvenuti, 1986). Yet, most of the participants reported our schools are failing to provide counseling. When asked "Did you feel safe discussing the issue of homosexuality with any adults at school?" only eight young women reported they had and in just two cases the adult was their counselor. Others reported: "There was nothing in the counselor's office dealing with gay issues that I ever saw" (D., 17, Pasadena, Texas). "I knew that my principal and guidance counselor were the wrong people to go to. I felt that they would offer me more problems than I needed" (K., 19, Batesville, Indiana). "I don't talk to my counselor much, because the counselors are so overloaded with kids that they only have time for disciplinary problems" (F., 17, Orange County, California). ". . . When I found out my sister was gay, I did talk about it with my guidance counselor and her attitude was alright, but she confessed to me that it disgusted her" (S., 19, Hartford, Wisconsin).

In summary, one participant's advice to counselors is, "just to be tolerant and vocal about their acceptance of homosexuality so that kids would know they had someone to talk to if they needed it" (D., 17, Monroe County, New York).

The Impact of Homophobia and Heterosexism on Sexual Minority Youth

There are many consequences to the cognitive, social, and emotional isolation which sexual minority youth experience as a result of homophobia and heterosexism. The results of this exclusion and stigmatization of sexual minority youth include social alienation; low self-esteem; drop-out risk and educational failure; and depression and suicide (Friend, 1993; Gibson, 1989; Herdt, 1989; Herdt & Boxer, 1993; Heron, 1994; Hetrick & Martin, 1988; McManus et al., 1991; Savin-Williams, 1990; Governor's Commission on Gay and Lesbian Youth, 1993; Uribe & Harbeck, 1992). Some sexual minority youth display other symptoms. They may hide their sexual orientation by losing themselves in their academic, athletic, and extracurricular pursuits (Sears, 1992).

Social Alienation. Almost all high school students experience high school as a social rather than an academic organization (Coleman, J. S., 1961; Cusick, 1973; Gordon, 1957). Many lesbian and gay students report feeling alienated in school (Governor's Commission on Gay and Lesbian Youth, 1993; McManus et al., 1991). These feelings were shared by many of the participants: "My worst memory is being asked to the dances and not going because no females had the nerve to ask me nor did I to ask them" (L., 15, Wayne, West Virginia).

Other participants shared their alienation:

> Last year, when I was in eleventh grade, I really began to feel different. I got really depressed, and had very low self-confidence. I thought I was the most hideous creature on earth, I drifted away from my friends. I thought they hated me. (D., 17, Monroe County, New York)

> The biggest problem for me has been the loneliness. Because I'm Chinese as well makes me feel even more isolated. Being Chinese and gay puts me into a unique position. My parents are very traditional and even though the general attitude towards gays has become more liberal over the past few years, my parents discount it and put it down as 'American craziness'. . . . I really would like to have had lesbian friends during my high school career. (F., 17, Orange County, California)

> Generally, I don't like high school. My most common feelings are unhappiness and resentment. I'm always like, why do I have to be here? This is stupid, they're not teaching this stuff

for me. That's it, I feel very much like none of this is done for me. I don't want to go to the prom. I don't want to learn how to raise a child or be married, I don't want to go cheer for the football team. That isn't my life. (M., 17, Montgomery County, Pennsylvania)

My worst memory is being lonely for so very long and no one caring or even really noticing. (S., 19, Madison County, Indiana)

Overall School Performance. Feelings of isolation and alienation in school often cause sexual minority youth to perform poorly or to drop out of school. This was not the case in this study. All of the participants are still in school. Though four participants reported having difficulty concentrating on their school work, the majority excelled in school. A few reported difficulties:

. . . well, the fact that I was struggling with my orientation definitely impacted my performance. I was so immersed in answering this "question" that it influenced the papers I wrote, the studying time I had, everything. I thought about it almost all the time and wondered about my teachers and if any of them were gay or the kids in my classes. . . . I tried to run away from my thoughts by not going home and hanging out with my friends all the time, so I didn't do all my homework and I hardly ever studied for anything. I got good grades anyway. (K., 21, Norfolk County, Massachusetts)

At first no [sexual orientation didn't impact my school work], but now that I feel the need to come out of the closet I get so tuned out that my grades and attendance have dropped. (L., 15, Wayne, West Virginia)

Most of the participants reported excelling in school. A number described burying themselves in their academic, athletic, and extra-curricular pursuits.

I was an extreme over-achiever. I partly feel I was like this to please my parents . . . so that they would see when I did come

out that gays weren't all bad ppl. [people] who they must fear
. . . but actually their own daughter . . . who did very well in
school and was a good person as well . . . (D., 17, Pasadena,
Texas)

Depression and Suicide. The typical stresses of adolescence take
on added dimensions for sexual minority youth. They struggle with
all the pressures that their heterosexual peers face in addition to a
hostile world that fears and rejects them (Kissen, 1991). Lesbian,
gay and bisexual youth internalize society's homophobia (McManus et al., 1991).
Silence and indifference to the destruction caused by homophobia lead to isolation, depression, and all too often suicide. Suicide or
attempted suicide is a common response to the discrimination
which sexual minority youth endure (Gibson, 1989; Remafadi, Farrow, & Deisher, 1991; Rofes, 1983).
Though I made no direct reference to isolation, depression or
suicide in my interviews, many young women chose to share their
experiences of anguish. "I really have no best memory of high
school. My worst memory was my suicide attempt my junior year"
(K., 19, Batesville, Indiana).
Other participants spoke about their feelings:

[It was at] the beginning of my junior year. It was after I came
out to myself, but before I came out to anyone else. I was
depressed a lot, and starting distancing myself from my friends
because I thought they'd reject me if they knew. I got really
concerned with my physical appearance, afraid that I wasn't
feminine enough and that people would figure it out. (A., 17,
Georgia: 9th grade–Forsyth Co.; 10th grade–Dawson Co.;
11th grade–Oconee Co.)

. . . in December of 1993, I tried to kill myself. School, parents, and my girlfriend breaking up with me just finally wore
me out and I hit rock-bottom. I was/am highly sensitive and I
needed someone to talk to about the problems I was having
with my girlfriend, and when she finally left me, I never felt so
alone in my life. I couldn't talk to anyone. (F., 17, Orange
County, California)

High school was a lonely place where I was different and usually unliked. People didn't like me because I was smart, over-weight, and different in my ideas. . . . I excelled in academics but I was alone for three of the four years of high school. When I found a friend, I found more and had to confront my sexuality and that added more pressure. At times it made me nearly suicidal and very depressed. I would not say that high school years are the best of my life. (S., 19, Madison County, Indiana)

Combating Heterosexism and Homophobia

In concluding the interviews, I invited the young women "to offer any advice for educators dealing with sexual minority students." Their responses offer perhaps the most valuable information this study has to contribute. The participants proposed the following actions to help combat heterosexism and homophobia in schools: "Be understanding about how much harassment they may get if they come out. High school is a cruel place sometimes" (A., 19, North Carolina). ". . . Accept the kids and their sexuality, otherwise, the depression and suicides are on your shoulders" (K., 19, Batesville, Indiana).

Other participants suggested:

- don't make the generalizations that all females date males and vice versa
- if they are gay and willing to listen to a student who may need their support, be vocal. Or if being vocal is not possible at least tell the guidance counselors that if a student comes in questioning their sexuality, or have realized it and need someone to talk to that you will do the job
- don't allow your students to get away with making discriminatory remarks about anyone!!
- encourage the libraries to begin or expand their collection of gay books
- celebrate pride week as you would celebrate black history month or presidents day or spirit week. Take pride in who you are

- fight to allow same sexed couples to the prom and all dances, etc. . . . (R., 19, Fairfield County, Connecticut)

My advice to educators is to bring homosexuality in as something natural, to confront student slurs, to open it up to discussion and work on breaking down stereotypes while kids are still formulating the dogma they'll carry forever! (R., 20, Montgomery Co., Maryland; and Montezuma, New Mexico)

Educators: Don't beat around the bush, get the subject out there, create an environment where questions can be answered correctly. Listen. Ask if you think someone might need to talk. (W., 19, New England)

I wish they would be more open to it and not sweep it under the rug. They should offer support, not add to the denial. (E., 19, Harris, Texas)

REFERENCES

Benvenuti, A. (1986). *Assessing and addressing the special challenge of gay and lesbian students for high school counseling programs.* Paper presented at the Annual Meeting of the California Educational Research Association. (ERIC Document Reproduction Service No. ED 279958).

Cass, V. C. (1984). Homosexual identity formation: A theoretical model. *Journal of Homosexuality, 4,* 219-235.

Coleman, E. (1988). *Integrated identity for gays and lesbians: Psychotherapeutic approaches for emotional well-being.* The Harrington Park Press.

Coleman, J. S. (1961). *The adolescent society: The social life of the teenager and its impact on education.* New York, NY: The Free Press.

Cusick, P. A. (1973). *Inside high school: The student's world.* New York, NY: Holt, Rinehart, and Winston, Inc.

Friend, R. (1993). Choices, not closets: Heterosexism and homophobia in schools. In L. Weis & M. Fine (Eds.), *Beyond silenced voices* (pp. 209-235). Albany, NY: SUNY Press.

Gibson, P. (1989). Gay male and lesbian youth suicide. In M. Feinleib (Ed.), *Report of the Secretary's Task Force on Youth Suicide, Vol. 3: Prevention and intervention in youth suicide.* (pp. 3-110). Washington, DC: U.S. Department of Health and Human Services.

Gordon, C. W. (1957). *The social system of the high school: A study of the sociology of adolescence.* Glenco, IL: The Free Press.

Governor's Commission on Gay and Lesbian Youth. (1993). *Making schools safe for gay and lesbian youth. Breaking the silence in schools and in families.* (Publication No. 17296-60-500-2/93-C.R.) Boston, MA: Author.

Herdt, G. (Ed.). (1989). *Gay and lesbian youth.* New York: The Haworth Press, Inc.

Herdt, G., & Boxer, A. (1993). *Children of horizons: How gay and lesbian teens are leading the way out of the closet.* Boston, MA: Beacon Press.

Heron, A. (Ed.). (1994). *Two teenagers in twenty: Writings by gay and lesbian youth.* Boston, MA: Alyson Publications, Inc.

Hetrick, E. S., & Martin, A. D. (1988). *Hetrick-Martin Institute violence report.* New York: The Institute for the Protection of Lesbian and Gay Youth.

Kaplan, S., & Saperstein, S. (1985). Lesbian and gay adolescents. In H. Hidalgo, T. L. Peterson, & N. J. Woodman (Eds.), *Lesbian and gay issues: A resource manual for social workers* (pp. 17-20). Silver Spring: National Association of Social Workers, Inc.

Kissen, R. M. (1991, November). *Listening to gay and lesbian youth.* Paper presented at the Annual Meeting of the National Council of Teachers of English, Seattle, WA. (ERIC Document Reproduction Service No. ED 344 220).

Lorde, A. (1983). There is no hierarchy of oppression. In L. Gordon (Ed.), *Bulletin on Homophobia and Education, 14* (3/4), 9.

Martin, A. D. (1982). Learning to hide: The socialization of the gay adolescent. In S.C. Feinstein, J.G. Looney, A. Schwartzberg, & J. Sorosky (Eds.), *Adolescent Psychiatry: Developmental and Clinical Studies* (Vol X) (pp. 52-65). Chicago: University of Chicago Press.

McManus, M. C., Asher, G., Bloodworth, R., Chambers, J., Fulmer, S., Goldberg, E., Hinds, E. A., Holloway, M. S., & Stutesman, D. (1991). *Oregon's sexual minority youth; An at-risk population. Lesbian, gay and bisexual youth.* Portland, OR: Task Force on Sexual Minority Youth.

Mercier, L. R., & Berger, R. M. (1989). Social service needs of lesbian and gay adolescents: Telling it their way. In P. Allen-Meares & C. H. Shapiro (Eds.), *Adolescent Sexuality: New challenges for social work* (pp. 75-95). New York: The Haworth Press, Inc.

O'Conor, A. (1993-94, October-January). Who gets called queer in school? Lesbian, gay and bisexual teenagers, homophobia and high school. *High School Journal, 77* (1-2), 7-12.

Proctor, C. D., & Groze, V. K. (1994, September). Risk factors for suicide among gay, lesbian and bisexual youths. *Social Work, 39* (5), 504-513.

Reed, D. B. (1992, October). *Gay youth in American public high schools: Invisible diversity.* Paper presented at the Annual Meeting of the University Council for Educational Administration, Minneapolis, MN. (ERIC Document Reproduction Service No. ED 354 438).

Remafedi, G. (1987). Homosexual youths: A challenge to contemporary society. *Journal of the American Medical Association, 258* (2), 222-228.

Remafedi, G., Farrow, J., & Deisher, R. (1991). Risk factors for attempted suicide in gay and bisexual youth. *Pediatrics, 87*(6), 869-875.

Rodgers, M. (1994). Growing up lesbian: The role of the school. In D. Epstein (Ed.), *Challenging lesbian and gay inequalities in education* (pp. 31-48). Buckingham, England: Open University Press.

Roesler, T., & Deisher, R. (1972). Youthful male homosexuality. *Journal of the American Medical Association, 219*, 1018-1023.

Rofes, E. (1983). *I thought people like that killed themselves: Lesbians, gay men and suicide.* San Francisco: Grey Fox Press.

Savin-Williams, R. C. (1990). *Gay and lesbian youth: Expressions of identity.* New York: Hemisphere Publishing Corp.

Schneider, M. (1989). Sappho was a right-on adolescent: Growing up lesbian. In G. Herdt (Ed.), *Gay and lesbian youth* (pp. 111-130). New York: The Haworth Press, Inc.

Sears, J. (1992). Educators, homosexuality and homosexual students: Are personal feelings related to professional beliefs? In K. Harbeck (Ed.), *Coming out of the classroom closet* (pp. 29-79). New York: The Harrington Park Press.

Troiden, R. R. (1988). *Gay and lesbian identity: A sociological analysis.* New York: General Hall Inc.

Unks, G. (1993-94, October-January). Thinking about the homosexual adolescent. *High School Journal, 77* (1-2), 1-6.

Uribe, V. (1991). *Project 10 handbook: Addressing lesbian and gay issues in our schools. A resource directory for teachers, guidance counselors, parents and school-based adolescent care providers.* Third edition. Los Angeles: Friends of Project 10, Inc.

Uribe, V., & Harbeck, K. (1992). Addressing the needs of lesbian, gay, and bisexual youth: The origins of Project 10 and school-based intervention. In K. Harbeck (Ed.), *Coming out of the classroom closet* (pp. 9-28). New York: The Harrington Park Press.

Learning Lessons from School: Homophobia, Heterosexism, and the Construction of Failure

Kathryn Herr

SUMMARY. Gay and lesbian youth drop out of school in disproportionate numbers. In tracing the school experiences of a young lesbian, this manuscript explores how heterosexism and homophobia contribute to the construction of a school "failure." It makes the point that what is construed as a "private problem," i.e., one young lesbian dropping out of school, is in reality a socially constructed issue that needs to be addressed on a level beyond that of the individual. *[Article copies available for a fee from The Haworth Document Delivery Service: 1-800-342-9678. E-mail address: getinfo@haworth.com]*

The theme of student invisibility has become a popular metaphor in educational writing as more researchers are viewing schools as consisting of multiple realities in which some realities are "defined out" of the dominant social construction (Anderson, 1990; Anderson & Herr, 1993). The lived experiences of gay and lesbian youth in schools are perhaps the most elusive; rendered invisible through the stigma attached to their identification as sexual minorities, they

Kathryn Herr, PhD, LISW, is affiliated with University of New Mexico, College of Education, Department of Language, Literacy and Sociocultural Studies, Hokona Hall 203, Albuquerque, NM 87131. E-mail: kherr@unm.edu

[Haworth co-indexing entry note]: "Learning Lessons from School: Homophobia, Heterosexism, and the Construction of Failure." Herr, Kathryn. Co-published simultaneously in *Journal of Gay & Lesbian Social Services* (The Haworth Press, Inc.) Vol. 7, No. 4, 1997, pp. 51-64; and: *School Experiences of Gay and Lesbian Youth: The Invisible Minority* (ed: Mary B. Harris) The Haworth Press, Inc., 1997, pp. 51-64; and: *School Experiences of Gay and Lesbian Youth: The Invisible Minority* (ed: Mary B. Harris) The Harrington Park Press, an imprint of The Haworth Press, Inc., 1997, pp. 51-64. Single or multiple copies of this article are available for a fee from The Haworth Document Delivery Service [1-800-342-9678, 9:00 a.m. - 5:00 p.m. (EST). E-mail address: getinfo@haworth.com].

are conveniently forgotten by the institutions charged with facilitating their education (Durby, 1994). While discourses regarding diversity and multiculturalism gain ground within school reform, the views of young gays and lesbians are noticeably absent and there is no equivalent groundswell within the adult community soliciting their voices. As a result, ". . . neither our school districts nor the gay and lesbian community have made significant progress in addressing the educational and social service needs of these young people" (Rofes, 1989, p. 450).

Fullan (1991) has made the point that research on organizational change and school life reveals a serious lack of studies concerning the subjective aspects of the school experience. Without access to the lived experience of students, those who design and implement practices and polices for schools devise well-intended reforms and interventions; they may or may not address the concerns of the constituencies which are supposedly being addressed.

This manuscript, drawing on indepth qualitative interviews, presents the narrative of one young lesbian, Elise; it specifically focuses on her experiences interfacing with the school environments she encountered before finally dropping out of high school and obtaining her GED. In attending closely to her story, we have the opportunity to draw from her experiences tentative recommendations that may serve well this previously ignored population.

THE SOCIAL CONSTRUCTION OF HETEROSEXISM AND HOMOPHOBIA

The experiences of gay and lesbian students need to be framed within a larger societal context where both heterosexism and homophobia are understood as social constructs that perpetuate patriarchy. Heterosexism is the belief that everyone should be heterosexual or what Audre Lorde (1984) describes as a "belief in the inherent superiority of one pattern of loving and thereby its right to dominance" (p. 45). One implicit role of societal institutions, such as schools, is to promote the pervasive ideology of heterosexism and thereby perpetuate clear constructs of maleness and femaleness. Friend (1993) observes that the roots of heterosexism are in sexism, with one of the purposes being to create boys and girls who grow up to be "real" men and women.

Homophobia, the fear of being gay and hatred of gays and lesbians, is a primary barrier to achieving gender equity. This fear of being thought to be gay or lesbian maintains traditional gender-role behaviors and enforces sexist behaviors and heterosexual privilege (Elia, 1993; Friend, 1993). To "fit into" schools and society in their current form is to accept, or at least not overtly resist, a privileging of some groups over others, in this case, a patriarchal arrangement.

THE CURRENT CONTEXT OF SCHOOLING FOR GAY AND LESBIAN STUDENTS

Actively ignored by educators (Sears, 1992), gay and lesbian youth are thought to be perhaps the most underserved of all students in our school systems (Uribe, 1994). This sense of being invisible within the borders of the schoolyard has been well documented (Durby, 1994; Rofes, 1989; Sears, 1993).

Friend (1993) sees homophobia and heterosexism shaped and reinforced in schools by two "interrelated mechanisms of silencing" (p. 212): systemic exclusion and systemic inclusion. The former is the process of excluding positive role models, messages, and images of gays and lesbians, rendering them invisible. In systemic inclusion, when discussions regarding gays and lesbians do occur, they are consistently placed in a negative context, linking homosexuality to pathology or dangerous behaviors. These techniques of silencing help to create the climate whereby tacit approval is given for antigay violence to take place in schools. They also reflect and reinforce heterosexist beliefs and attitudes.

While the actual percentage of lesbian, gay, and bisexual students remains indeterminable, some estimates put their numbers at up to ten percent of the student body (Durby, 1994). Despite their numbers, for many young gays and lesbians, school is a lonely place (Elia, 1993; Uribe, 1994). Depending on the climate in any given school, gay and lesbian students may not self-identify or have any type of organized coalition within the confines of the school environment that would support a gay identity.

One reason for not publicly identifying as gay in school is the high number of incidents of harassment and abuse perpetuated on gay students by their student peers (Savin-Williams, 1995). They are also probably the most frequent victims of hate crimes (Friend, 1993). While educators increasingly interrupt racist discourses in school, they are still unlikely to "hear" or comment on remarks expressed by students or professional peers that are derogatory to young gays and lesbians.

In addition, information and positive images of gays and lesbians are routinely omitted from school curriculums (Rofes, 1989; Sears, 1993). The search for unbiased, accurate information regarding homosexuality is often a frustrating one for adolescents and one that is rarely successful in terms of resources located within the school environment (Uribe, 1994). As D'Augelli (1992) points out, young gays and lesbians are often "deleted" from the formal curriculum, yet the " 'hidden curriculum' that devalues the existence and con-tributions of lesbians and gay men is quite clear" (p. 214).

DEVELOPING A SENSE OF SELF IN THE SCHOOL CONTEXT

Gay and lesbian teenagers report that between ages 12 and 14 they became more aware that they were more attracted to persons of the same sex. Many gay and lesbian teenagers report that they somehow considered themselves outsiders or felt different for many years; for a large number this dated back to early childhood (Anderson, 1994; Savin-Williams, 1995).

Ages 12 to 14 are likely to coincide with middle school. This is a time psychosocially when students are preoccupied with being part of a peer group; through the formation of a sense of belonging to a group, students eventually proceed toward more of an individual sense of self. Toward the end of their middle school years and as they enter high school, adolescents are typically addressing the question "Who am I?" Part of the goal of the developmentally appropriate school environment during these years is to provide a richness of information and opportunities as adolescents try on possible selves and possible futures.

Unfortunately for gay and lesbian adolescents, schools are often another place where they face overt rejection (Telljohann & Price,

1993) or an impenetrable silence that lets them know their identity as a sexual minority is either a taboo topic or unacceptable. Misinformed adults, perhaps well-intended, reassure gay and lesbian students that their sense of being gay is a passing phase (Durby, 1994; Elia, 1993; Uribe, 1994); this reframing of their experiences, seen through a heterosexist lens, devalues the meaning making of the gay or lesbian student while offering a more "appropriate" alternative explanation. The hostility of an environment that would erase them impacts the gay or lesbian adolescent's developing sense of self, potentially creating a negative self-appraisal and providing a clear obstacle to the integration of a positive self-identity.

Hetrick and Martin (1987, cited in Mallon, 1994) point out that, in addition to the usual developmental tasks of adolescence, the primary task for young gays and lesbians is adjustment to a socially stigmatized role. It is the *social stigma* related to being gay or lesbian that may be injurious to positive identity development in the young adolescent.

At a time in their lives when they should be freely exploring "Who am I?", young gays and lesbians instead are encouraged to either hide their sexual orientation or attempt to change themselves into acceptable heterosexuals; the third option, that of openly accepting themselves as gay or lesbian, is the most optimal and the one least encouraged by society (Mallon, 1994). Of course the same cultural context that would encourage a young adolescent to be closeted is the same one that violently harasses the openly gay or lesbian adolescent.

> . . . they are doubly victimized–by the homophobia of their social worlds and by the myths they have internalized. In this process of oppression, they have been implicitly told that their development is abnormal and their prospect for personal and family fulfillment is slight. In this sense, they have been deprived of their own development. (D'Augelli, 1992, p. 214)

As gay and lesbian students work to make meaning of a school world that seemingly includes no one like themselves–no visible, adult, gay role models, no positive images or curriculum that would offer a window into the worlds of sexual minorities–they are in danger of concluding "that they can have no future, no vision, no role models, no possibilities" (Jackson & Sullivan, 1994, p. 98). Not finding themselves in school, they leave in disproportionate numbers (Elia, 1993).

The following portrait of Elise unpacks this individual problem-solving in an attempt to move these issues from the "personal" to public spheres; in doing so, what was formerly "personal" and "individual" is reconceptualized as first a societal and then an institutional issue demanding broader, public interventions. Commonly when young gay and lesbian students struggle, we make them the focus of our professional interventions; in reconceptualizing the issue, the homophobia and heterosexism inherent in our culture, in our professions, and in ourselves become the targets for change.

CONSTRUCTING A SCHOOL "FAILURE"

I first met Elise several years ago when she was about to turn 17. This was an important birthday for her, demarcating an opportunity to leave school "for real" and take the GED. She could make official the school leavetaking behaviors that she had been practicing for several years. In elementary school she had been in programs for the gifted but by high school she was failing miserably.

Barely five feet tall, with sparkling gray-blue eyes, this young Anglo woman had come out as a lesbian at 14. While there was incredible relief at being able to name herself aloud to herself and others, she had also publicly owned being a sexual minority; as such, she was put at risk by the societal baggage that comes with this identity.

In the medium-sized urban area in which she lives, Elise is a known activist, an outspoken advocate for gay and lesbian youth issues. For example, she has frequently been asked to speak at gatherings for educators, social workers, and school counselors, addressing issues of gay and lesbian adolescents. To see her in action in these public forums is to be very impressed; she fields informational questions as well as hostile remarks with seeming ease. An articulate, forceful speaker, she is open about her own struggles as a young lesbian as well as her own experiences in school that eventually led to her dropping out. Now 19 years old, she currently supports herself waitressing in a local cafe; this job is one in a series of minimum wage jobs that she has landed since getting her GED.

This particular paper then attempts to understand the climate of school for a young lesbian and why, after years of being unable to bring herself to school, she finally dropped out. At the heart of the paper is a paradox: How is it that a young student as vibrant and bright as Elise can't "make it" in school?; what is the climate we have created that conveys to Elise that there is no room for her in school? Three themes drawn from interviews with Elise work to address these questions as well as some beginning interventions; the following sections address issues of curriculum, of adult modeling, and finally, the translation of issues of heterosexism and homophobia into a "personal problem" for gay and lesbian youths.

BEING RENDERED INVISIBLE IN THE CURRICULUM

In Elise's school experiences, curriculum that supported heterosexism was demonstrated both explicitly in what was being taught and implicitly in what was taboo. The combination of the two resulted in gay and lesbian students being left out of the public discourse, rendering them invisible. This maintenance of their invisibility is seen as part of a heterosexist agenda that continues to privilege "the inherent superiority of one pattern of loving." As Elise describes it:

> Everyone is required, freshman year, to take health class. They get into the *logistics* even of heterosexual sex, safe sex, etc. etc. Uhm and it had about two sentences on homosexuality and I read those same two sentences over and over and over again, hoping to extract some hidden meaning, something from them. It said 'Some people,' and I believe the wording was '*choose* to have relationships, have sex, something, with people of the same sex; these people are called homosexuals.' That was *it* . . . the stuff they were teaching us in health class had *absolutely nothing* to do with what I was going through.

The lack of relevant information in the explicit curriculum was mirrored in the cultural messages surrounding her that conveyed to

Elise that being lesbian was at the very least negative if not deviant. While the explicit curriculum had very little to say about being gay in school, the hidden curriculum said a lot. Most explicitly what it taught was that it was not safe to be gay. She concluded this because there were no "out" gay teachers and because harassment of students thought to be gay went on uninterrupted. There were so many instances of being harassed that Elise came to think of it as the norm.

NO ONE TO TURN TO

While rendered invisible by the formal curriculum, and encouraged to be invisible by the harassment of the hidden one, Elise was also without adult role models or relationships that could help her find some alternative, positive spaces within the school environment. Teachers that she knew to be gay portrayed themselves as heterosexuals and while Elise understood their fear in being thought gay, she also felt that students, herself included, "are needing their help."

> I mean I would never out them to any of the students . . . because that was their business and not my business. But that I knew and they would be there talking about their heterosexual lifestyle . . . it seemed like almost, like a lot of them were anti-gay or that's how they acted . . . they were so afraid of people finding out that they went in completely the opposite direction.

The homophobia that keeps gay and lesbian adults in the closet also effectively isolates gay youth from open, positive role models. What they see modeled instead is that hiding their gay identities and "passing" as heterosexuals is one way to survive a hostile culture. As long as gays and lesbians are effectively hidden, the heterosexist culture can proceed unchallenged.

Some adults in the school, perhaps misinformed themselves, passed this misinformation on to Elise. She told the following story with great relish, while also aware that if she had not been so clear in her own lesbian identity, the damage could have been much greater.

I came out to my counselor in my freshman year in high school. I've told this story over and over because it cracks me up but it's also very scary. It's just that she told me first of all not to confuse being gay with masturbation. Uh, which confused me. I wasn't confused before (laughs) but I was after that. She said 'Don't let your gay friends pressure you into it.' At this point in time I knew I was gay; I recognized that fact but I didn't have any gay friends. Nobody's pressuring me into it; I don't know any gay people–that's why I'm upset. 'Don't make a decision like this until you're at least 18.' . . . I was in there saying I'm gay, not I *think* I'm gay . . . I believe if I had not been secure in already recognizing who I was and very strong-minded . . . that would have probably pushed me back in the closet. If this wasn't misinformation . . .

The guidance counselor persisted in not hearing Elise even when presented with her truths. The research would tell us that this counselor is not unusual in that many mental health professionals are not prepared, or are poorly prepared, to meet the needs of gay and lesbian youth (Murphy, 1992).

A Private Problem

When students cannot find themselves in the explicit curriculum, and with no one to turn to in the school, they are left without accurate and positive information from which to make meaning of their experiences, thoughts, and feelings. This implicitly translates what is a public problem, i.e., the fact that not everyone is represented positively in the school and social environment, to a private issue, i.e., how am I to understand who I am as a sexual minority?

I always knew that I had an attraction toward women but I never thought of it as being normal; I thought I was the only one that ever felt like this. This is all through growing up, all through childhood . . . I thought I would grow up and marry a man and have kids and that I'd be miserable. Or I thought my only other alternative was having a sex change even though I didn't feel like a male and I didn't want to be a male, but that was the only way I could feel happy and be with a woman. So with those two as my options, or what I thought was my only options, . . . I was really, really depressed. Because I didn't really look forward to either of those . . .

With no images of possible lives she might live, Elise was left alone to make meaning of the experience of being gay. After weeks of attempting to "come out," she finally talked with her mother. With her help, Elise discovered a youth group at the Gay and Lesbian Community Center and began going. For Elise, to find other gay and lesbian youth was a transforming experience:

I was so happy actually to realize that—oh wow, it's very difficult to describe the feeling—realizing, feeling completely completely alone and then realizing that other people know exactly where you're at or what you're going through. I mean it was amazing.

But since the gay community she was finding for herself did not overlap with her school experience, Elise continued to be very isolated at school. Having gotten a sense of support and community, the isolation at school became increasingly intolerable.

I found my life completely outside of school—other people like myself, meaning gay, in the community outside of school— women's events, activities I volunteered for outside of school. All of this stuff that my social life revolved around had absolutely nothing to do with high school . . .

While finding a place outside of school provided a lifeline for Elise, the upshot of not finding herself in school resulted in failing grades.

You know I went from straight A's in elementary school to decent in middle school and then to just absolutely pretty much failing in high school. A lot of it was because my focus was not on high school. I don't think it was that I was stupid in any way . . . I knew I had no motivation because it wasn't my place, . . . to be alone in a bunch of heterosexual people is an uncomfortable feeling because there isn't really anybody else who knows what you're going through or what's going on, at least in the gay sense.

Elise did eventually drop out, but not without a sense of regret as to what she thought it might have been like should she have been able to find herself in school:

> It's kind of like missing out on a part of your childhood . . . I missed out on elementary school, middle school and high school–on those experiences that could have been wonderful . . . instead of all that, I was giving myself ulcers. I was in elementary school and middle school and ended up dropping out of high school. And it's all because of my sexuality.

And while the school system failed Elise, she is left to wonder if she is the failure:

> It is a big blow to the self-esteem in terms of oh I couldn't hack it in high school. And even though that's not true–like you said I aced the GED, it was easy– . . . there's still this feeling of guilt and self-doubt which was like 'Okay, I couldn't handle it in high school.' And because my grades did slip in high school because of . . . all the problems I was having, I felt like I'm dumb; I'm not good enough to do this. So there was a lot of, a lot of self-doubt and uhm, I beat myself up quite a bit over it.
>
> I personally–especially after realizing how much better things got after I got out of high school–I personally think the GED, there's nothing wrong with it. But there's still also a stigma attached to the GED . . . that it's kind of like the losers' way out.

While acting on her own behalf both in finding community and in leaving a school environment that felt hostile to her, Elise is still left with the difficulty of overcoming the feelings of failure at not being able to hack it. This sense of failure has kept her from going on with her education; college currently feels out of the question for her. And given her previous experiences in the school system, it makes a tragic kind of sense to avoid further experiences in it.

DISCUSSION

When Elise left school, she experienced a distinct sense of well-being, relief from an environment where she was alternately invisible, harassed, "wrong," or misunderstood. This is consistent with Fine's (1991) finding that many dropouts from school, moving away from an environment they find hostile, initially feel a sense of relief, exhilaration, and well-being; within three or four years of leaving school this sense of well-being diminishes and is replaced with self-blame, depression, and a sense of diminished life chances. What initially then was a move toward self-preservation and health, in the long run extracts a high price in terms of a positive sense of self. Elise's own struggle is to hold onto the fact that she is bright and "breezed through the GED" while wondering if she has taken the "losers' way out."

In imagining a school experience where she would have seen herself in the curriculum, with openly gay and lesbian role models, or with adults to talk honestly with, Elise says:

> That would have made the most amazing difference . . . reducing that feeling that I was a freak and that I was the only one. Would have helped me realize that this is cool; there are people who live their lives like this . . . I think it would have taken a lot of that depression away, a lot of that anxiety, that fear.

What is so important about Elise's experience is that she names for us that, in her experience, school is a fearful, anxiety-producing place for a young lesbian; she gives voice to the experience of other young gays and lesbians who leave school in numbers disproportionate to their representation. There were several crucial arenas in Elise's school experience when the adult professionals in her school environment could have made a vast difference. Certainly in terms of sculpting an inclusive curriculum, in interrupting harassment, and in correcting stereotypes and misinformation, adults could have had a valuable part; all of these areas are ones that professionals on the "front lines" have some control of to a certain degree.

To use these discretionary powers on behalf of gay and lesbian youth, we would first need to educate ourselves to the issues and deal with our own responses to sexual minorities. We would have to be willing to interrogate our own practices and interrupt our own heterosexist biases or homophobic beliefs. All of this is to actively translate Elise's "private problem" into a school and societal issue as well as a personal one for professionals working in schools. While the negative experiences of gays and lesbians in schools are in part unique, they can also be seen as the result of an overall effort to maintain traditional gender-roles and (hetero)sexist arrangements that privilege patriarchy. The focus for active intervention, then, moves beyond Elise and her own experience of school to one of creating a climate where not only gay and lesbian youth can be safe and thrive but also others disenfranchised in the current arrangements of school and society can be included.

What we come to know, through narratives such as Elise's, is that current societal beliefs and practices collude to produce school. For schools and educators to challenge the kind of tunnel vision that flattens out rich differences will require a level of activism and advocacy that is not currently present. But should we choose those roles, to use Elise's terminology, now that could "make an *amazing* difference."

REFERENCES

Anderson, D. A. (1994). Lesbian and gay adolescents: Social and developmental considerations. *The High School Journal, 77*, (1/2), 13-19.

Anderson, G.L. (1990). Toward a critical constructivist approach to school administration: Invisibility, legitimation, and the study of non-event. *Educational Administration Quarterly, 26*, (1), 38-59.

Anderson, G.L., & Herr, K. (1993). The micro-politics of student voices: Moving from diversity of bodies to diversity of voices in schools. In C. Marshall (Ed.), *The new politics of race and gender* (pp. 58-68). Washington, D.C.: Falmer Press.

D'Augelli, A. R. (1992). Teaching lesbian/gay development: From oppression to exceptionality. In K. M. Harbeck (Ed.), *Coming out of the classroom closet: Gay and lesbian students, teachers, and curricula* (pp. 213-227). Binghamton, NY: The Haworth Press, Inc.

Durby, D. (1994). Gay, lesbian and bisexual youth. In T. DeCrescenzo (Ed.), *Helping gay and lesbian youth: New policies, new programs, new practice* (pp. 1-37). New York: The Haworth Press, Inc.

Elia, J. P. (1993). Homophobia in the high school: A problem in need of a resolution. *The High School Journal, 77*, (1/2), 177-185.

Fine, M. (1991). *Framing dropouts: Notes on the politics of an urban public high school*. Albany, NY: SUNY Press.

Friend, R. A. (1993). Choices, not closets: Heterosexism and homophobia in schools. In L. Weis & M. Fine (Eds.), *Beyond silenced voices: Class, race, and gender in US schools* (pp. 209-235). Albany, NY: SUNY Press.

Fullan, M. (1991). *The new meaning of educational change.* New York: Teachers' College Press.

Jackson, D., & Sullivan, R. (1994). Developmental implications of homophobia for lesbian and gay adolescents: Issues in policy and practice. In T. DeCrescenzo (Ed.), *Helping gay and lesbian youth: New policies, new programs, new practice* (pp. 93-109). New York: The Haworth Press, Inc.

Lorde, A. (1984). *Sister outsider.* Freedom, CA: The Crossing Press.

Mallon, G.P. (1994). Counseling strategies with gay and lesbian youth. In T. DeCrescenzo (Ed.), *Helping gay and lesbian youth: New policies, new program, new practice* (pp. 75-91). New York: The Haworth Press, Inc.

Murphy, B. C. (1992). Educating mental health professionals about gay and lesbian issues. In K. Harbeck (Ed.), *Coming out of the classroom closet: Gay and lesbian students, teachers and curricula* (pp. 229-246). Binghamton, NY: The Haworth Press, Inc.

Rofes, E. (1989). Opening up the classroom closet: Responding to the educational needs of gay and lesbian youth. *Harvard Educational Review, 59* (4), 444-453.

Savin-Williams, R. C. (1995). Lesbian, gay male and bisexual adolescents. In A. R. D'Augelli & C. J. Patterson (Eds.), *Lesbian, gay and bisexual identities over the lifespan: Psychological perspectives* (pp. 165-189). New York: Oxford University Press.

Sears, J. T. (1992). The impact of culture and ideology on the construction of gender and sexual identities: Developing a critically based sexuality curriculum. In J. Sears (Ed.), *Sexuality and the curriculum: The politics and practices of sexuality education* (pp. 139-156). New York: Teachers College Press.

Sears, J. T. (1993). Alston and Everetta: Too risky for school. In R. Donmoyer & R. Kos (Eds.), *At-risk students: Portraits, policies, programs and practices* (pp. 153-172). Albany, NY: SUNY Press.

Telljohann, S.K., & Price, J.H. (1993). A qualitative examination of adolescent homosexuals' life experiences: Ramifications for secondary school personnel. *Journal of Homosexuality, 26* (1), 41-56.

Uribe, V. (1994). The silent minority: Rethinking our commitment to gay and lesbian youth. *Theory into practice, 33* (3), 167-172.

Beyond High School:
Heterosexuals' Self-Reported
Anti-Gay/Lesbian Behaviors and Attitudes

Amy M. Rey
Pamela Reed Gibson

SUMMARY. This study examined interpersonal heterosexist discrimination by examining self-reported anti-gay behaviors of heterosexual college students. Respondents were 226 college students; 94.9% had perpetrated some form of discriminatory behavior and 32.7% had committed a behavior that was rated as moderately harmful or higher. A higher amount of self-reported discriminatory behavior was associated with being male, having more homophobic attitudes, and having lower GPAs. Discriminatory behaviors were not related to political ideology, religious influence, or interaction with gay men and lesbians. Neither discriminatory behaviors nor homophobic attitudes were related to academic year, age, membership in a social fraternity/sorority, or membership on an intercollegiate athletic team. *[Article copies available for a fee from The Haworth Document Delivery Service: 1-800-342-9678. E-mail address: getinfo@haworth.com]*

It is widely recognized and understood that lesbians and gay men are a persecuted minority in this nation, but their victimization by

---

Amy M. Rey and Pamela Reed Gibson are both affiliated with the Department of Psychology, James Madison University, Harrisonburg, VA 22807. E-mail Dr. Gibson at: gibsonpr@jmu.edu

[Haworth co-indexing entry note]: "Beyond High School: Heterosexuals' Self-Reported Anti-Gay/Lesbian Behaviors and Attitudes." Rey, Amy M. and Pamela Reed Gibson. Co-published simultaneously in *Journal of Gay & Lesbian Social Services* (The Haworth Press, Inc.) Vol. 7, No. 4, 1997, pp. 65-84; and: *School Experiences of Gay and Lesbian Youth: The Invisible Minority* (ed: Mary B. Harris) The Haworth Press, Inc., 1997, pp. 65-84; and: *School Experiences of Gay and Lesbian Youth: The Invisible Minority* (ed: Mary B. Harris) The Harrington Park Press, an imprint of The Haworth Press, Inc., 1997, pp. 65-84. Single or multiple copies of this article are available for a fee from The Haworth Document Delivery Service [1-800-342-9678, 9:00 a.m. - 5:00 p.m. (EST). E-mail address: getinfo@haworth.com].

heterosexuals is often misunderstood and underestimated. In recent years harassment and violence against gay men and lesbians has been recognized as a serious social problem (Jenness, 1995), partially as a result of better data collection and documentation of anti-gay incidents.

Between 1991 and 1994 anti-violence projects in five cities gathered information about 6,861 anti-gay incidents, the majority of which were not reported to the proper authorities (Conaty, 1996). The high incidence of hate crimes led to the 1990 Hate Crime Statistics Act, which requires the federal government to gather data on bias crimes. Since its passage the FBI has documented a total of 25,439 hate-motivated crimes (Conaty, 1996). In a report to the National Institute of Justice, Finn and McNeil (as cited in Berrill & Herek, 1990) state that gay men and lesbians are probably the minority most frequently victimized by hate violence.

Incidents of abuse or attack on lesbians and gay men have been labeled as hate or bias crimes, defined by Herek (1989) as ". . . words or actions intended to harm or intimidate an individual because of her or his membership in a minority group" (p. 948). These crimes are damaging because they are, symbolically, assaults on a whole group of individuals. They not only affect one member of the group, attacking his or her identity, but also create a climate of fear and intimidation for the entire minority or class of people (Herek, 1989). Given the number of crime victims and the devastating consequences of these crimes, research is needed to understand who perpetrates these acts and why and to suggest solutions for anti-gay discrimination, harassment, and violence.

The victimization of homosexuals can take many forms, including isolation, loss of a job or legal rights, verbal harassment, threats of violence, property damage, or in many cases, actual physical attack. Lott and Maluso (1995) distinguished between institutional discrimination and interpersonal discrimination. Institutional discrimination refers to the exclusion of a minority group within the context of social institutions, for example, making same-sex marriages illegal or denying custody or visitation to homosexual parents. Interpersonal discrimination is excluding, avoiding, and distancing minority persons on a more interpersonal, direct level. Lott and Maluso (1995) stressed that these two types of discrimination are inexorably bound, and that all interpersonal discrimination takes place within the greater framework of the institutional discrimination that pervades society.

Fernald (1995) defined interpersonal heterosexist discrimination as ". . . face to face overt behaviors that distance, avoid, exclude, or physically violate lesbians or gay men" (p. 82). She explained that minor incidents, derogatory comments, for example, occur with much greater frequency than outright violence and physical assault. This study focused on interpersonal heterosexist discrimination, which ranges from purposefully ignoring to violently assaulting a lesbian or gay man.

CONSEQUENCES OF VICTIMIZATION

Homosexual crime victims must, especially if their attack involved a perpetrator's knowledge of their homosexuality, deal with the stigma of being a homosexual in a predominantly heterosexual culture. All anti-gay attacks occur in the context of a heterosexist society. Herek (1990) defines heterosexism as ". . . an ideological system that denies, denigrates, and stigmatizes any non-heterosexual form of behavior, identity, relationship, or community" (p. 316). When gay men or lesbians are in some way assaulted, and this includes verbal harassment and isolation, they are faced with the heterosexist notion that their homosexuality, a part of their identity, is sick, wrong, and deserving of punishment (Garnets, Herek, & Levy, 1992).

Most anti-gay crime, including verbal or physical assaults, goes unreported (D'Augelli, 1992; Herek, 1989, 1993; Norris, 1992; Pilkington & D'Augelli, 1995). In fact, Herek (1993) found that 90% of the 166 gay men, lesbians, and bisexuals he studied at Yale University who had experienced some form of threat, harassment, or violence did not report at least one incident. Victims' reasons for not reporting include fear of harassment from authorities, minimization of the importance of the incident, fear of public exposure, and the belief that nothing could be done about the incident (D'Augelli, 1992; Herek, 1993; Norris, 1992).

INCIDENCE OF VICTIMIZATION

Berrill (1990) compared the results of ten different studies conducted by anti-violence organizations or government agencies that examined reports by gay men and lesbians about their experiences as victims of anti-gay abuse. Berrill summarized that between 58% and 87% of participants reported experiencing verbal abuse; 24%-48% reported threats of violence; 12%-20% reported property damage; 21%-27% reported objects thrown at them; 13%-38% reported being followed or chased; 7%-15% reported being spat upon; 9%-23% reported being punched, kicked, or hit; and 4%-10% reported being assaulted with a weapon.

A number of studies have investigated anti-gay victimization in high school and college students. Pilkington and D'Augelli (1995) studied 194 gay, lesbian, and bisexual youths between the ages of 15 and 21 from 14 different communities around the nation. The sample included 142 males and 52 females. Participants in the study were asked if they had experienced various types of abuse as a result of someone knowing or assuming they were homosexual. The reported incidence was as follows: 80% reported verbal insults; 44% reported threats of attack; 23% reported vandalism; 33% reported objects thrown at them; 31% reported being chased or followed; 13% reported being spat upon; 18% reported physical assault; 9% reported being assaulted with a weapon; and 22% reported sexual assault. More than three quarters (83%) of the participants said they had experienced at least one form of victimization, and on average they experienced 2.7 forms.

Hunter (1990) conducted a study of 500 youths who sought help at an agency in New York City that provides services for gay and lesbian youths and their families. She found 40% had experienced violent attacks, 46% of which were said to be anti-gay. Hunter found a higher percentage of anti-gay violence within the family (61%) than did other researchers (reviewed by Comstock, 1991), possibly because youths often contact the institute for help with problems in the home.

Several studies have examined the incidence of anti-gay victimization on college campuses (Cavin, 1987, cited in Comstock, 1991; D'Augelli, 1992; Norris, 1992). Herek (1993) examined 166 gay men, lesbians, and bisexuals at Yale University and found the following percentages of victimization: 65% reported verbal insults; 25% reported threats of violence; 19% reported objects thrown at them; 10% reported property damage; 25% reported being chased or followed; 5% reported being beaten; 3% reported being spat upon; 1% reported being assaulted with a weapon; and 12% reported sexual harassment or assault.

PERPETRATORS

Perpetrators and potential perpetrators have not been studied as a population; thus the number of victimizers in the general population is unknown (Comstock, 1991). A tentative profile of perpetrators of these kinds of acts has been developed, but this profile is based almost entirely on victims' reports. It is important to gather information on victimizers by studying populations of heterosexuals to determine who commits anti-gay behaviors and why.

Weissman (1992) and Collins (1992) studied perpetrators of anti-gay crime in interviews and journalistic accounts. Weissman found a group of middle class high school and college students who were engaged in simple recreation and were influenced by peer pressure. They also felt that society, in part, condoned their behavior. Collins identified a rough group of white supremacist, working-class men who were out to prove their manhood by defeating what is "anti-male" (Collins, 1992, p. 195). Neither account identified a large sample or used empirical evaluation, but both provided self-reports from victimizers.

Explanations of perpetrator motivation. There are various theories regarding the motivations of those who victimize gay men and lesbians. Ehrlich (1990) recognized that so much victimization is unreported that most available information is based on a biased sample of victim reports. He concluded, therefore, that it is difficult to identify who perpetrators are and why they do what they do, because we know very little about them directly.

Ehrlich (1990) believed that much of the interpersonal discrimination of gay men and lesbians is instrumental, or that it serves some purpose or function for the perpetrator. He theorized that one such function is the gain of power and control which is evoked by violations of territory or property, violations of sacred cultural values, and violations of status. Another purpose this victimization can serve is to fulfill a need for affiliation and social conformity; homosexuals violate the norm, and acting out against them reaffirms one's connections with others in the in-group.

Herek (1990) agreed with Ehrlich (1990) that interpersonal heterosexist discrimination serves a purpose, and he identified three separate functions of victimizing gays and lesbians. First he identified a value-expressive function which allows one to affirm oneself by displaying important internal values which are seen as reflecting identity. Second, anti-gay victimization can have a social-expressive function by allowing one to gain approval and esteem from significant others. Finally, anti-gay prejudice can have a defensive function which relates to unconscious conflicts. In other words, an individual may commit anti-gay acts as a way of maintaining her or his heterosexuality and denying her or his own internal conflicts or homosexual feelings.

Harry (1990) sees anti-gay violence as an end in itself; he does not believe that it serves any distinct purpose. Harry feels that groups of young males get together to express hedonism and autonomy. These anti-gay acts are an attempt to prove bravery and manhood and are simply a rebellion against social order that does not entail severe negative consequences.

PURPOSE

This study was an attempt to identify the frequency and context of interpersonal heterosexist discrimination in a sample of college students by examining self-reports of heterosexuals. Both the incidence of anti-gay behavior and the situations and motivations which surround it were studied. Also, an attempt was made to discover what demographic variables are related to discriminatory behavior.

Although this is preliminary and exploratory research, several hypotheses were proposed: (1) Heterosexist attitudes, as measured by Herek's (1994) Attitudes Toward Lesbians and Gay Men (ATLG) scale would be correlated with incidence of heterosexist discriminatory behaviors; (2) There would be differences in discriminatory attitudes and behaviors related to gender, amounts of interaction with gay men and lesbians, religious influence, and political ideology. These demographics have previously been related to homophobic attitudes: Kite and Whitley (1996) found that men had significantly more homophobic attitudes than women; Whitley (1990) found that knowing gay men and lesbians was related to a decrease in homophobic attitudes; McFarland (1989) found that fundamental religious beliefs were positively correlated with homophobic attitudes; and Herek (1988), using the same scale used in this study, found a correlation between political ideology and anti-gay attitudes.

METHOD

Participants

Participants were taken from two computerized random samples, one of 750 first year students and one of 750 seniors at a mid-sized Mid-Atlantic university. Students were reached by telephone and asked to respond to a mail survey, and the first 250 from each class to agree were sent surveys and return envelopes. Of the 593 students who were reached by phone, 15 refused to participate in the study. Of the 578 persons contacted by phone who agreed to participate, 209 returned their surveys (return rate of 36.2%). An additional 43 first year students volunteered through the psychology department subject pool bulletin board, all of whom completed the survey. Twenty-six participants were eliminated because they were not heterosexual or were not seniors or first year students, which brought the total number of participants utilized in the study to 226.

Measures

The first questions in the survey were designed to measure demographic variables including gender, age, race/ethnicity, and others.

The Discriminatory Behaviors Scale (DBS) was designed for this study to measure behaviors associated with interpersonal heterosexist discrimination, including harassment, violence, and isolation. A focus group of gay men and lesbian college students ($N = 12$)

weighted individual items on the scale, according to their perception of how damaging each item would be. These weights were used to group and rank items on a scale ranging from one to four with one being "minimally harmful," two "moderately harmful," three "very harmful," and four "severely harmful." Those weights (listed in Table 1) were then multiplied by the frequency of the behavior, from zero to three with zero being "never," one "once," two "twice," and three "three or more times" to compute a score on each item for each participant. The scores from each item were then added to create a final discriminatory behaviors score, which can theoretically range from zero to 184. There were also open-ended questions in the survey which asked participants to explain any anti-gay incidents, why they participated, and when they occurred.

Although some items on the DBS were designed by the researchers to measure milder anti-gay behavior, many items were similar to those included in surveys designed to measure victims' experiences (D'Augelli, 1992; Herek, 1993). All items were evaluated by the focus group of lesbian and gay students, and no members of the group felt that items were inappropriate or that the survey lacked important items; thus the DBS does have a degree of content validity. The DBS also had a satisfactory internal consistency ($\alpha = .7497$), but it was not ideal. This is possibly because the scale covered a wide range of items. Although most people responded that they had perpetrated the milder anti-gay behaviors, very few responded that they had done one of the more severe anti-gay behaviors.

The ATLG was designed by Herek (1994) to measure heterosexuals' attitudes toward homosexuals and consists of 20 items presented with a 9-point Likert scale ranging from "strongly disagree" to "strongly agree." Scores can range from 20 (positive attitudes) to 180 (negative attitudes). The ATLG can be divided into two subscales–Attitudes Toward Lesbians (ATL) and Attitudes Toward Gay Men (ATG). Herek (1994) found satisfactory internal consistency ($\alpha = .90$) with 368 undergraduate students and high internal consistency ($\alpha = .95$) with 405 students at six different universities. The two subscales of the ATLG were significantly correlated ($p < .05$) with construct validity measures.

TABLE 1. Frequencies of Discriminatory Behaviors Against Gay Men and Lesbians (g/l)

Behavior	Never involved in behavior	With others who did behavior	Did behavior
Minimally harmful			
Laughed at/agreed with jokes or derogatory statements	21 (9%)		205 (91%)
Made jokes or derogatory statements	65 (29%)		161 (71%)
Used terms "fag," etc.	43 (19%)		183 (81%)
Didn't befriend gay man	196 (88%)		28 (12%)
Didn't befriend lesbian	210 (93%)		15 (7%)
Made sexually explicit comments	159 (70%)	65 (29%)	12 (5%)
Moderately harmful			
Made jokes or derogatory statements in front of g/l	198 (88%)		28 (12%)
Used terms "fag," etc. in front of g/l	186 (83%)		39 (17%)
Purposely ignored	182 (81%)		44 (19%)
Excluded from an activity	213 (94%)		13 (6%)
Verbally harassed	165 (73%	59 (26%)	10 (4%)
Very harmful			
Ended friendship	225 (100%)		1 (0%)
Tried to convince others not to befriend	216 (96%)		10 (4%)
Threatened with violence	207 (92%)	19 (8%)	1 (0%)
Chased or followed	226 (100%)	0 (0%)	0 (0%)
Vandalized home or property	225 (100%)	1 (0%)	0 (0%)
Severely harmful			
Assaulted with a weapon	226 (100%)	0 (0%)	0 (0%)
Punched, kicked, hit, etc.	222 (98%)	3 (1%)	2 (1%)
Coerced or forced into sexual activity	221 (98%)	5 (2%)	0 (0%)

Note. All percentages were rounded to the nearest integer. Some participants both committed a behavior and were with others who committed a behavior, so rows may not add to 100%. Blank cells indicate that data were not collected for the item.

Procedure

Students who agreed to complete the survey were mailed or given the survey and a cover letter. The cover letter explained that participation was voluntary, that the participant could withdraw from the study at any time, and that participation implied consent. There was nothing to connect participants' names with their responses, and in data analysis only numbers were used to identify surveys. SPSS for Windows was used to analyze the collected data.

RESULTS

Of the 226 participants, 110 (48.7%) were male and 116 (51.3%) were female; 107 (47.3%) were freshmen and 119 (52.7%) were seniors; 208 (92%) were Caucasian, 7 (3.1%) were African-American, 7 (3.1%) were Asian-American, 2 (.9%) were Latino/Latina, and 2 (.9%) classified themselves as other.

All tests in this study were conducted at the $p = .01$ level of significance. Potential differences between mail survey and subject pool participants were examined with t-tests. No differences were found with regard to sex, GPA, political ideology, religious influence, membership in a social fraternity or sorority, membership on an intercollegiate sports team, number of gay male friends, number of lesbian friends, ATLG score, and Discriminatory Behaviors score. The data from the two groups were therefore analyzed together.

Incidence and Explanation of Discriminatory Behaviors

The number of discriminatory behaviors that participants admitted to was calculated to establish the overall prevalence of discrimination. The numbers of individuals who were involved in each behavior, and the weight from 1 (minimally harmful) to 4 (severely harmful) assigned to each behavior are described in Table 1. Only 12 individuals (5.1%) did not commit any discriminatory behaviors, and 73 individuals (32.7%) committed at least one discriminatory behavior that was weighted moderately harmful or higher.

Twenty participants (8.8%) responded that they had committed at least one of the following behaviors: made sexually explicit comments; verbally harassed; threatened with violence; chased or followed; vandalized home or property; punched, kicked, or beat; assaulted with a weapon; or coerced or forced into sexual activity. Of those 20, 11 reported that the behavior occurred before college. Persons reported making sexually explicit comments in elementary school ($n = 2$), middle school ($n = 2$), and high school ($n = 7$). Persons reported verbally harassing in elementary school ($n = 1$), middle school ($n = 2$), and high school ($n = 7$). One person each reported vandalizing property and physically assaulting, both in high school.

Twenty-four participants responded to the question regarding motivations for anti-gay behaviors. The motivations participants listed for anti-gay behavior were: joking, entertainment, or "something to do" ($n = 14$); not approving of homosexuality or because the person looked or acted gay ($n = 7$); anger or malicious intent ($n = 4$); a need for acceptance or peer pressure ($n = 3$); because he felt he was being "checked out" ($n = 1$).

Respondents' Perceptions of the Effects of Discrimination

A number of participants reported laughing at or initiating jokes about gay, lesbian, and bisexual (g/l/b) students in the schools, but denied that it did any harm. Several participants reported that the joking was not malicious, and that it was done only in the presence of heterosexuals and therefore did not hurt the feelings of any lesbian or gay male students. For example, one respondent reported that she had "made verbal comments/jokes among a group of friends–never directly to a person to hurt them." Respondents also denied that comments were in any way connected to their own actual feelings regarding homosexuality: "I might not even think about it when I say the word 'Dyke' or etc. This by no means describes how I feel about homosexuality."

Other comments reflected the idea that differences are fair game for humor, and should not be taken seriously. One respondent said:

> I have used the terms homo, queer, fag, faggot, and made jokes about homosexuality among heterosexuals only because we

were all joking around or because my friends and I always crack on folks and each other about religion, sexuality, ethnicity, and other such because we all think it's funny and people take it too seriously.

Similarly, one respondent said that "People who take serious offense to jokes need to lighten up–the world works easier that way–less stress, etc."

One respondent prided himself on the fact that his verbal harassment, even when it was directed toward a particular person, did not escalate to physical harm. After describing continued verbal harassment of a male student perceived to be gay by a group of male students in the high school cafeteria, he said:

[N]ever, however, did any physical abuse occur. This was a Catholic School, the administration would never intervene in the name-calling but physical abuse would not be tolerated. Besides I have more class than that. As a post-script to this story, our taunting eventually drove him out of our school.

ATLG and DBS Scores

The mean ATLG score was 81.40 ($SD = 34.03$), with a mean ATL of 35.69 ($SD = 17.85$) and a mean ATG of 45.27 ($SD = 17.65$). Respondents seem to have more homophobic attitudes toward gay men than toward lesbians, which is consistent with Herek's (1994) finding. The ATL and ATG were analyzed separately from the ATLG for this study, but because there were no unique relationships involving the subscales, those results were not included. The mean DBS score was 10.11 ($SD = 8.30$).

On the ATLG, males ($M = 91.62$, $SD = 30.43$) had significantly higher scores than females ($M = 72.12$, $SD = 34.59$), t (206) = 4.297, $p < .001$. Also on the DBS, males ($M = 13.91$, $SD = 9.28$) had significantly higher scores than females ($M = 6.60$, $SD = 5.26$), t (165) = 7.303, $p < .001$.

Participants who had few or no gay male friends had higher ATLG scores ($M = 84.83$, $SD = 33.58$) than those who had three or more gay male friends ($M = 58.37$, $SD = 27.91$), t (138) = 4.876, $p < .001$, and participants who had few or no lesbian friends had higher ATLG scores (M = 84.74, SD = 33.00) than those who had three or more lesbian friends (M = 55.75, SD = 31.43), t (150) = 4.448, p < .001. There were no differences found on the DBS scale as a function of the participant's number of gay male or lesbian friends.

Correlations were performed to establish the relationship between anti-gay attitudes and behaviors and their relationship to religious influence, political ideology, and GPA. The ATLG scores were positively correlated with religious influence (N = 222, r = .316, p < .01) and conservative political ideology (N = 207, r = .534, p < .01). The DBS scores were positively correlated with GPA (N = 212, r = .210, p < .01). ATLG and DBS scores were also positively correlated with each other (N = 206, r = .349, p < .01).

Using t-tests, we found no significant differences in means on the ATLG or DBS scores as a function of academic year, age, membership in a social fraternity or sorority, or membership on an intercollegiate athletic team.

DISCUSSION

Frequencies of Discriminatory Behaviors

The results of this study indicate that most heterosexual university students report involvement in a substantial amount of interpersonal heterosexist discrimination. The majority of participants (71%) admitted to joking and making derogatory statements and using slurs like "fag," "queer," and "dyke" (81%). Respondents tended to minimize the extent to which their actions were personally damaging to gay men and lesbians. A number of participants also admitted to more severe behaviors, including verbal harassment, making sexually explicit comments, and physical violence, most of which occurred before college.

Although the frequency of discrimination is sizeable, these numbers seem low when one considers the level of discriminatory behaviors reported by gay men and lesbian victims (D'Augelli, 1992; Herek, 1993; Norris, 1992). One or more of the following may be relevant here: (1) some persons who participated in discriminatory behaviors may not have returned the survey; (2) many who did respond may not have admitted committing negative behaviors; (3) persons who reported engaging in behaviors "three or more times" may have offended any number of people; thus a small number of offenders may account for a large amount of discrimination. Therefore, frequencies reported here may be a very conservative estimate.

ATLG and DBS Scores

As predicted, the ATLG scores were correlated with gender, political ideology, religious influence, and interaction with gay men and lesbians. The DBS scores were not, however, related to these variables, with the exception of gender. It seems that many of the influences on behavior and attitude are not the same. Part of this difference might be explained by the fact that attitudes may change throughout life–i.e., one may not presently feel the same about gay men and lesbians as at age eight–and the ATLG scores should reflect current attitudes. However, we asked participants about any anti-gay behavior, whether it occurred recently or in childhood, and so the DBS score would reflect both current and past actions. Comparing current attitudes and current behaviors might yield higher correlations.

It was hoped that this study might identify variables related to anti-gay behavior. Although, as predicted, homophobic attitudes do correlate with discriminatory behaviors and are obviously a relevant factor in predicting anti-gay behavior, there are other important predictors of behavior. It can be concluded, however, that perpetrators tend to be male, to be more homophobic, and to have lower GPAs.

Other factors may cause a person to convert negative attitudes into anti-gay behavior. Perhaps personality characteristics such as aggression or lack of social inhibitions are necessary to incite a person to discriminatory behavior. It is also possible that anti-gay behavior has a separate motivation, and is not dependent on attitude or belief: it could be a way of asserting one's membership in the in-group (Ehrlich, 1990); of gaining approval from one's peers

(Herek, 1990); or of expressing rebellion and youthful hedonism (Harry, 1990).

Implications for School Environments

The high number of college students who reported having been present for or engaging in verbal harassment of gays and lesbians in early, middle, and high school has implications for the school climate for youth who do not identify with a heterosexual orientation. Although a number of respondents claimed that their negative comments about g/l/b students were made only in the presence of heterosexuals, the assumptions are (1) that the students can tell who is heterosexual, and, (2) that random comments in the school environment do not harm anyone to which they are not specifically targeted. Comments, jokes, and laughter about sexual orientation can create a negative climate for g/l/b students, whether or not they are open about their orientation. It is obvious from their comments that many heterosexual students are either ignorant about or reluctant to admit the effects of their harassment.

Although it is well established that adult gays and lesbians are as well adjusted as heterosexuals, g/l/b adolescents do show some adjustment difficulties including an elevated risk of suicide (Hunter, 1990). A negative school climate is a probable contributor to these problems. Savin-Williams (1994) reviewed studies suggesting that harassment contributes to school problems such as failure, truancy, dropping out, and suicide attempts. An oppressive school environment may prevent g/l/b youths from experiencing a complete adolescence in regard to early relationships (Coleman, 1982), and "contaminates the process of adolescent identity formation" (Malyon, 1982, p. 60). See Morrow (this volume) for an in-depth discussion of the problems in identity development faced by g/l/b students in the schools.

Although Miranda and Storms (1989) found a positive relationship in adults between lesbian/gay identity formation and psychological adjustment, youths who do self-label or self-disclose (thus pursuing a g/l/b identity), or who are more obvious about their sexual orientation, report experiencing higher levels of victimization (Pilkington & D'Augelli, 1995). Perhaps because of this, most g/l/b students do not disclose their sexual orientation in school (Harris & Bliss, this volume).

Citing victimization and other risks for g/l/b youths, the American Psychological Association Policy Statement on Lesbian and Gay Issues (APA, 1991) mandates that:

> The American Psychological Association and the NASP [National Association of School Psychologists] support providing a safe and secure educational atmosphere in which all youths, including lesbian, gay, and bisexual youths, may obtain an education free of discrimination, harassment, violence, and abuse, and which promotes an understanding and acceptance of self. (p. 9)

This atmosphere will be established only through broad interventions that target the harassers and those responsible for supervising the school climate. See Fontaine (this volume) for suggestions for creating more hospitable school environments for g/l/b students. Friend (1993) has described an intensive training program for educators that addresses sexism, racism, heterosexism, and ableism and is facilitated by a team diverse in gender, ethnicity, sexual orientation, and able-bodiedness. In addition to giving attention to the attitudes, values, and feelings of the participants, the program encourages proactive strategies on the part of the school for integrating g/l/b concerns in the curriculum. Friend describes some positive results of the program and concludes that ". . . if educators choose to do nothing, they must be willing to be held accountable for supporting school environments in which lesbian, gay, and bisexual students often drop out, act out, commit suicide, or survive physically while losing self-esteem . . ." (p. 66). The incident in the high school cafeteria described earlier in this paper reflects what happens to g/l/b youth in the schools when schools "do nothing" and echoes Weissman (1992) in that the school milieu seemed to condone this acting out. A passive stance on the issue of treatment of g/l/b students in the schools perpetuates abuse and increases the number of students that arrive on college campuses with no more tolerant attitudes than they held in middle and high school regarding sexual orientation.

Limitations of the Present Study

The first limitation of this study relates to possible response bias in the sample as a result of using a mail survey. The surveys were mailed in groups over a four month period and over a long break in the university schedule, which could have caused varying response rates for different groups. Also, it is possible that those who are the most homophobic and the most serious perpetrators of anti-gay behavior would be the least willing to complete a survey dealing with homosexual issues. However, those who completed the survey through the subject pool, none of whom refused to participate, did not differ significantly on measures of behavior or attitude.

Another limitation relates to the DBS. This is a new scale, and further analysis is necessary, including evaluation of test-retest reliability. Also, higher internal consistency might be achieved by developing two or more separate scales to measure different levels of anti-gay behavior. Although, as expected, the DBS was moderately correlated with the ATLG, further analysis should be conducted into the construct validity of the DBS measure.

Finally, the population of college students may be relatively homogeneous in regards to anti-gay behavior. Education level may be negatively correlated with heterosexist discrimination, as it is with homophobic attitudes (Herek, 1988).

FUTURE RESEARCH

Further research should be conducted about the frequency of victimization from the perpetrator's viewpoint. Replicating this study with in-person interviews instead of mail surveys may increase knowledge and open up further avenues of study. It would also be helpful to study different populations, as college students severely minimize generalizability.

Studying students in elementary, middle, and high schools may yield interesting and important results because much of this discrimination takes place in primary and secondary schools. By studying this population, researchers may be able to uncover information regarding origins and motivations for such behavior which could be used to design intervention at a primary prevention stage.

Exploration of other variables that might predict anti-gay behavior, including personality characteristics and other values and beliefs may also be useful. Also, uncovering motivations for discriminatory behaviors will probably lead to a better understanding of how to combat anti-gay violence and discrimination.

REFERENCES

American Psychological Association policy statements on lesbian and gay issues. (1991). Committee on Lesbian and Gay Concerns. American Psychological Association.

Berrill, K.T. (1990). Anti-gay violence and victimization in the United States: An overview. *Journal of Interpersonal Violence, 5*(3), 274-294.

Berrill, K.T., & Herek, G.M. (1990). Violence against lesbians and gay men: An introduction. *Journal of Interpersonal Violence, 5*(3), 269-273.

Coleman, E. (1982). Developmental stages of the coming out process. In J. Gonsiorek (Ed.), *Homosexuality and psychotherapy: A practitioner's handbook of affirmative models* (pp. 31-43). New York: The Haworth Press, Inc.

Collins, M. (1992). The gay-bashers. In G.M. Herek & K.T. Berrill (Eds.), *Hate Crimes: Confronting violence against lesbians and gay men* (pp. 191-200). Newbury Park: Sage Publications.

Comstock, G.D. (1991). *Violence against lesbians and gay men.* New York: Colombia University Press.

Conaty, T. (1996). Statement submitted by the National Gay and Lesbian Task Force in support of legislation to permanently authorize the Hate Crime Statistic Act 1. Internet address: http://www.ngtlf.org/pub.html.

D'Augelli, A.R. (1992). Lesbian and gay male undergraduates' experiences of harassment and fear on campus. *Journal of Interpersonal Violence, 7*(3), 383-395.

Ehrlich, H.J. (1990). The ecology of anti-gay violence. *Journal of Interpersonal Violence, 5*(3), 259-365.

Fernald, J.L. (1995). Interpersonal heterosexism. In B. Lott & D. Maluso (Eds.), *The social psychology of interpersonal discrimination* (pp. 80-117). New York: The Guilford Press.

Friend, R. (1993). Undoing homophobia in schools. *The Education Digest, 58*(6), 62-66.

Garnets, L., Herek, G.M., & Levy, B. (1992). Violence and victimization of lesbians and gay men: Mental health consequences. In G.M. Herek & K.T. Berrill (Eds.), *Hate crimes: Confronting violence against lesbians and gay men* (pp. 207-226). Newbury Park: Sage Publications.

Harry, J. (1990). Conceptualizing anti-gay violence. *Journal of Interpersonal Violence, 5*(3), 350-358.

Herek, G.M. (1988). Heterosexuals' attitudes toward lesbians and gay men: Correlates and gender differences. *Journal of Sex Research, 25,* 451-477.

Herek, G.M. (1989). Hate crimes against lesbians and gay men: Issues for research and policy. *American Psychologist, 44*(6), 948-955.

Herek, G.M. (1990). The context of anti-gay violence: Notes on cultural and psychological heterosexism. *Journal of Interpersonal Violence, 5*(3), 316-333.

Herek, G.M. (1993). Documenting prejudice against lesbians and gay men on campus: The Yale Sexual Orientation Survey. *Journal of Homosexuality, 25*(4), 15-30.

Herek, G.M. (1994). Assessing heterosexuals' attitudes toward lesbians and gay men. In B. Greene & G. M. Herek (Eds.), *Lesbian and gay psychology* (pp. 206-228). Thousand Oaks: Sage Publications.

Hunter, J. (1990). Violence against lesbian and gay male youths. *Journal of Interpersonal Violence, 5*(3), 295-300.

Jenness, V. (1995). Social movement growth, domain expansion, and framing processes: The gay/lesbian movement and violence against gays and lesbians as a social problem. *Social Problems, 42*(1), 145-170.

Kite, M.E., & Whitley, B.E., Jr. (1996). Sex differences in attitudes toward homosexual persons, behaviors, and civil rights: A meta-analysis. *Personality and Social Psychology Bulletin, 22,* 336-353.

Lott, B., & Maluso, D. (1995). Introduction: Framing the questions. In B. Lott & D. Maluso (Eds.), *The social psychology of interpersonal discrimination* (pp. 1-11). New York: The Guilford Press.

Malyon, A. (1982). Psychotherapeutic implications of internalized homophobia in gay men. In J. Gonsiorek (Ed.), *Homosexuality and psychotherapy: A practitioner's handbook of affirmative models* (pp. 59-69). New York: The Haworth Press, Inc.

McFarland, S.G. (1989). Religious orientations and the targets of discrimination. *Journal for the Scientific Study of Religion, 28,*(3), 324-336.

Miranda, J., & Storms, M. (1989). Psychological adjustment of lesbians and gay men. *Journal of Counseling and Development, 68,* 41-76.

Norris, W.P. (1992). Liberal attitudes and homophobic acts: The paradoxes of homosexual experience in a liberal institution. *Journal of Homosexuality, 22*(3-4), 81-120.

Pilkington, N.W., & D'Augelli, A.R. (1995). Victimization of lesbian, gay, and bisexual youth in a community setting. *Journal of Community Psychology, 23*(1), 34-56.

Savin-Williams, R.C. (1994). Verbal and physical abuse as stressors in the lives of lesbian, gay male, and bisexual youths: Associations with school problems, running away, substance abuse, prostitution, and suicide. *Journal of Consulting and Clinical Psychology, 62,* 261-269.

Weissman, E. (1992). Kids who attack gays. In G.M. Herek & K.T. Berrill (Eds.), *Hate crimes: Confronting violence against lesbians and gay men* (pp. 170-178). Newbury Park: Sage Publications.

Whitley, B.E., Jr. (1990). The relationship of heterosexuals' attributions for the causes of homosexuality to attitudes toward lesbians and gay men. *Personality and Social Psychology Bulletin, 16,* 369-377.

Coming Out in a School Setting: Former Students' Experiences and Opinions About Disclosure

Mary B. Harris
Gail K. Bliss

SUMMARY. The present study was conducted to learn more about the experiences of gay men and lesbians in educational settings, particularly about experiences relevant to disclosure of their sexual orientation. One hundred six gay men and 156 lesbian women responded to an anonymous questionnaire dealing with how their sexual orientation had affected their experiences in school.

As students, very few respondents had chosen to disclose their sexual orientation to principals, teachers, counselors, or friends. Reasons cited for nondisclosure included fear of the consequences and not wanting others to know. The majority of those who did disclose their sexual orientation received positive feedback for doing so, but respondents reported both positive and negative consequences of coming out. Gay men were aware of their sexual orientation at an earlier age than lesbians and were somewhat more likely to recommend disclosure to principals and teachers. Females were more likely to disclose only to females, whereas males were likely to come out to both males and females. Generally, the similarities between males and females were greater than the differences, with both

Mary B. Harris and Gail K. Bliss are both affiliated with the Department of Educational Psychology, College of Education, University of New Mexico, Albuquerque, NM 87131. E-mail Dr. Harris at: mharris@unm.edu

[Haworth co-indexing entry note]: "Coming Out in a School Setting: Former Students' Experiences and Opinions About Disclosure." Harris, Mary B. and Gail K. Bliss. Co-published simultaneously in *Journal of Gay & Lesbian Social Services* (The Haworth Press, Inc.) Vol. 7, No. 4, 1997, pp. 85-100; and: *School Experiences of Gay and Lesbian Youth: The Invisible Minority* (ed: Mary B. Harris) The Haworth Press, Inc., 1997, pp. 85-100; and: *School Experiences of Gay and Lesbian Youth: The Invisible Minority* (ed: Mary B. Harris) The Harrington Park Press, an imprint of The Haworth Press, Inc., 1997, pp. 85-100. Single or multiple copies of this article are available for a fee from The Haworth Document Delivery Service [1-800-342-9678, 9:00 a.m. - 5:00 p.m. (EST). E-mail address: getinfo@haworth.com].

groups being cautious about coming out in the school setting. *[Article copies available for a fee from The Haworth Document Delivery Service: 1-800-342-9678. E-mail address: getinfo@haworth.com]*

The existence, extent, and correlates of homophobia have been well documented in our society (Elia, 1993/94; Eliason, 1995; Harris & Vanderhoof, 1995; Herek, 1988; Herek & Capitano, 1996; Kielwasser & Wolf, 1993/94; Kite & Whitley, 1996; Kurdek, 1988; Whitley & Kite, 1995). Even health care professionals, who might be expected to be better informed than the general public, are not immune to such prejudice (Harris, Nightengale, & Owen, 1995). Moreover, the mainstream mass media can be a major contributor to heterosexism (Kielwasser & Wolf, 1993/94).

Although one might hope that educators would be models of enlightened thinking and that schools would be places in which prejudices would be examined rather than taught, it is more realistic and accurate to recognize that these negative attitudes are pervasive in schools as well (Anderson, 1994; Elia, 1993/94; Kielwasser & Wolf, 1993/94). Elia (1993/94, p. 179) states that "it could be argued that homophobia is more concentrated and more vicious in high schools than in any other institution." Crumpacker and Vander Haegen (1987, p. 65) add that "homophobic incidents abound on college campuses."

Even when homophobia is not overt, homosexuality may be a taboo topic and gays and lesbians may be invisible in schools. Teaching about homosexuality is specifically prohibited by law in many school systems, and textbooks either ignore or present misleading images of gays and lesbians (Anderson, 1994; Kielwasser & Wolf, 1993/94). When homosexuality is discussed it may be poorly handled (Telljohann & Price, 1993). Uribe and Harbeck (1991, p. 11) conclude that "Cultural taboos, fear of controversy, and a deep rooted, pervasive homophobia have kept the educational system in the United States blindfolded and mute on the subject of adolescent, educator, and parental homosexuality."

Because of the widespread prejudice against them (Elia, 1993/94; Harris & Vanderhoof, 1995; Herek, 1988; Herek & Capitano, 1996), many gays and lesbians have been socialized to conceal their homosexuality. Disclosing one's sexual orientation carries definite risks for individuals who do not fit the expected heterosexual pattern. These risks may be particularly great for students, the most numerous and the most vulnerable members of the educational community, since adolescence is a time when peer pressure is at its peak (Telljohann & Price, 1993) and when developing a sense of self is particularly important (Martin & Hetrick, 1988).

In order to be accepted by the peer group, many gay and lesbian adolescents choose to deny or hide their homosexuality rather than disclosing it to others (Elia, 1993/94; Martin & Hetrick, 1988). However, attempts to conceal their homosexuality may lead these youths to distance themselves from family and peers and may cause a reduction in self-esteem that continues with them into adulthood (Kielwasser & Wolf, 1993/94; Martin & Hetrick, 1988; Uribe & Harbeck, 1991). The need for concealment may partially explain why gay, lesbian, and bisexual youth face an increased risk of suicide, depression, truancy, dropping out of school, and other behavioral problems associated with increased stress and decreased self-esteem (Elia, 1993/94; Harbeck, 1993/94; O'Conor, 1993/94; Reynolds & Koski, 1993/94; Rofes, 1989; Telljohann & Price, 1993; Uribe, 1993/94).

The purpose of the present study was to add to the research on the consequences of coming out in school by using a relatively large sample of gay and lesbian adults who lived in a variety of areas and who responded to an anonymous questionnaire about their experiences in high school. They were asked about their decisions to disclose their sexual orientation or not, the reasons for their decisions, and (where relevant) the reactions of others to their coming out. We predicted that respondents would indicate a great deal of reluctance to reveal their sexual orientation to others in the educational system, particularly those with power over them such as peers, teachers, and principals. We also predicted that disclosure would lead to both positive and negative consequences.

Finally, since little research has compared the educational experiences of gay men and lesbians, differences between gay men and lesbians were examined. Some authors have suggested that prejudice is greater towards gay men than towards lesbians, particularly among males (Herek, 1988; Herek & Capitano, 1996; Kite & Whitley, 1996; Whitley & Kite, 1995). Elia (1993/94) indicated that this gender difference is found in high schools as well as society at large. However, the conclusion that more prejudice is directed towards gay males than towards lesbians is not accepted by all (Oliver & Hyde, 1993, 1995). Because of this lack of agreement, no predictions about gender differences were made.

METHOD

Participants

Participants were 106 men and 156 women who were vacationing in a town known for its heavy concentration of gay and lesbian residents and visitors. All identified themselves as homosexual (97%) or bisexual (3%). Their mean age was 37 years, with a range from 22 to 66. The typical respondent was Caucasian (88%), had at least a bachelor's degree (74%), had a professional occupation (54%), and came from the Northeastern part of the United States (73%), but all regions of the country were represented in the sample.

Procedure

Respondents were recruited by a lesbian graduate student at two locations frequented primarily by gay men and lesbians: a beach and a resort. Potential participants were asked if they would be willing to fill out a questionnaire dealing with the experiences of gay men and lesbians in the school system. After agreeing to participate, they were asked if they were a parent or a teacher. Those who said "yes" were given additional sections of the questionnaire that will not be discussed here.

Instrument

All participants responded to a four page structured questionnaire designed to explore issues related to coming out in the school setting. The questionnaire was attached to a cover letter which explained its purpose, provided names and addresses to contact for further information, and indicated that responding to the instrument implied consent for the researchers to analyze and use their responses. The first section of the questionnaire requested demographic information. The second section asked about their siblings and about the ages at which they suspected, were certain of, and disclosed to friends and family their sexual orientation. The third section of the instrument dealt with the respondents' experiences in high school, specifically whether, why or why not, and to whom they had disclosed their sexual orientation. It also asked about the reactions of others to this disclosure, in both structured and open-ended questions.

RESULTS

Participant Characteristics and Experiences

Table 1 presents some of the characteristics of the male and female respondents. As can be seen from the Table, gay males were significantly more likely than lesbians to be living alone. Lesbians were significantly more likely to be living with a same sex partner and living with children. Table 1 also presents the mean ages at which respondents suspected they were gay, were certain they were gay, and disclosed their homosexuality to parents, siblings, friends, and (when relevant) spouses. Independent samples t tests comparing males and females revealed that the male participants were significantly younger than the females and had suspected they were gay, known for certain that they were gay, and told their siblings and friends that they were gay at significantly younger ages than had the female participants. Males and females did not differ significantly with respect to ethnicity, religion or occupation (largest $\chi^2[5, N = 255] = 10.01, p > .05$).

Although 75% of the respondents had brothers and 65% had sisters, only 14% of them had gay or lesbian siblings. An even smaller percentage suspected (2.4%) or knew (.4%) that they had a parent who was homosexual. Males and females did not differ significantly on these dimensions (largest $\chi^2[3, N = 247] = 3.86, p > .05$).

Disclosure

Disclosure to principal. Only two of the respondents, both males, indicated that they had disclosed their homosexuality to the princi-

TABLE 1. Characteristics of Male and Female Participants

Living Arrangements[a]:	All Participants N = 258	Males N = 105	Females N = 153	χ^2
Living Alone	31%	40%	25%	6.69**
Living With Male Partner	14%	33%	1%	51.99***
Living With Female Partner	40%	6%	64%	88.06***
Living With Male Friend	9%	21%	1%	26.98***
Living With Female Friend	4%	3%	4%	.20
Living With Children	6%	1%	9%	7.64**

Ages:	All Participants M	N	Males M	N	Females M	N	t
Current Age	37	256	35	104	39	152	−4.40***
Age Suspected Gay	15	254	12	102	16	152	−5.32***
Age Certain Gay	21	247	18	99	22	148	−5.36***
Age Told Parents	26	170	25	75	26	95	−1.58
Age Told Siblings	26	168	24	64	27	104	−2.69**
Age Told Friends	24	254	22	104	25	150	−3.74***
Age Told Spouse	31	18	29	5	32	13	−.50

a. These categories are not mutually exclusive.
**$p < .01$ ***$p < .001$

pal of their high school, one at age 14 (grade 8) and one at age 16 (grade 12). The student who came out at age 14 reported the principal's reactions to be moderately supportive, slightly indifferent, moderately accepting, slightly confrontational, moderately uncomfortable, moderately reassuring, and moderately helpful. The other reported only that the principal "caught us having sex in elevator." He rated the principal as moderately accepting but did not respond to the other scales.

Table 2 presents the mean ratings of the importance of each reason for not disclosing one's sexual orientation to the principal, with 1 indicating "not at all" important and 5 indicating "extremely" important. As can be seen from the Table, the most important reason for nondisclosure was fear that others would find out, followed by not wanting parents to know, not seeing the need to

TABLE 2. Reasons for Not Disclosing One's Sexual Orientation

(Non) Disclosure to:	Principal		Teacher		Counselor		Friends	
Reason:	M^a	N	M	N	M	N	M	N
Fear of individual's reaction	3.26	122	3.54	106	3.17	101	4.26	80
Fear others would find out	4.06	125	4.13	108	3.80	104	4.31	81
Didn't see a need	3.78	120	3.71	101	3.71	105	3.32	71
Didn't want parents to know	3.97	127	4.08	104	3.86	101	3.74	74
Other reason	4.46	11	4.09	11	35.4	13	3.63	8

a. 1 = "not at all"; 5 = "extremely" important reason

disclose, and a fear of the reactions of others. Males and females did not differ significantly in the rated importance of any of these reasons (largest $t[123] = .96, p > .05$).

Disclosure to teacher(s). The majority of the respondents (86%) did not disclose their sexual orientation to any teachers. The reasons for their failure to disclose are given in Table 2. As can be seen from the Table, the primary reasons were fear that others would find out, not wanting their parents to know, not seeing a need to tell the teacher, and fear of the teacher's reaction.

Thirty-three of the participants said that they had disclosed their sexual orientation to teachers, at a median age of 18 years and a median grade level of 11th grade. Of these, 18 had come out to only one teacher and the rest to two or more. Most (22) had come out to a same sex teacher, but 8 had spoken to an opposite sex teacher and five had come out to both male and female teachers. A chi square test of independence revealed a statistically significant difference between males and females in the gender of the teachers to whom they disclosed ($\chi^2[2, N = 35] = 7.76, p < .05$). Males were equally likely to disclose only to male (36%) or only to female (36%) teachers, with 29% disclosing to teachers of both sexes, whereas females were far more likely to come out only to female teachers

(81%), with only 14% disclosing only to male teachers and 5% coming out to teachers of both genders.

The reactions of teachers to the student's disclosure are presented in Table 3. The mean reactions, which were not mutually exclusive, ranged from definitely supportive, accepting, and helpful through moderately reassuring to slightly indifferent, confrontational, and uncomfortable. Males and females did not differ significantly on any of the reactions received from teachers (largest $t[23] = 1.11$, $p > .05$).

Disclosure to counselor. As was true for teachers, most respondents (92%) did not report disclosing their sexual orientation to a counselor. Their reasons for nondisclosure, reported in Table 2, are similar to those for nondisclosure to principals and teachers: fear that others would find out, not wanting parents to know, not seeing a need to do so, and fear of the counselor's reaction.

The 17 respondents who said that they had come out of the closet to a counselor said that they had done so at ages ranging from 9 to 42 years. These responses imply that not all were referring to school counselors in answering this question. The mean ratings of those who responded suggest that they found the counselor to be moderately supportive, accepting, helpful, and reassuring and slightly indifferent, uncomfortable, and confrontational (see Table 3). There were no sig-

TABLE 3. Reactions to Disclosing One's Sexual Orientation

Disclosure to:	Teacher		Counselor		Friends	
Reaction:	M^a	N	M	N	M	N
Supportive	3.94	33	3.44	16	3.90	68
Accepting	3.83	29	3.31	16	3.85	65
Reassuring	3.33	27	2.63	16	3.08	60
Helpful	3.59	27	2.94	17	2.98	60
Indifferent	2.04	26	2.00	15	2.34	59
Uncomfortable	1.67	24	1.67	15	2.07	61
Confrontational	1.68	25	1.60	15	1.33	61

^{a}1 = not at all; 5 = extremely

nificant gender differences on any variables related to disclosure to counselors (largest $t[8] = -1.72, p > .05$).

Disclosure to friends. A substantially larger proportion of the respondents, although still a minority (36%), said that they had disclosed their sexual orientation to one (6%), two (7%) or more friends, at a median age of 17 years and a median grade level of 11th grade. The only significant gender difference was that females who came out to friends did so at a lower grade ($M = 10.5$) than did males ($M = 11.4$) ($t[44] = 2.40, p < .05$).

Of those who disclosed their sexual orientation to friends, 53% did so only to same sex friends, 7% only to opposite sex friends, and 41% to friends of both sexes. A chi square test of independence revealed that there were significant differences between males and females in the gender of the friends to whom they came out ($\chi^2[2, N = 76] = 6.55, p < .05$). Males were most likely to come out to friends of both sexes (54%), then to only males (39%), and then to females (8%); females were most likely to come out only to other females (68%), followed by friends of both sexes (27%), and by males (5%).

The reasons given for nondisclosure, seen in Table 2, are similar to the reasons for not disclosing to others at school: fear that others would find out, fear of friends' reactions, not wanting parents to know, and seeing no need to do so. For those who did disclose, the mean responses of friends, shown in Table 3, were generally positive: definitely supportive and accepting, moderately reassuring and helpful, slightly indifferent and uncomfortable, and not at all confrontational. No gender differences were found in these responses (largest $t[63] = 1.85, p > .05$).

Advice. Responses to the question, "Based on your experience, would you advise someone else to disclose their homosexuality to . . . ?" are provided in Table 4. As can be seen from the Table, most respondents did not advise disclosing to principals, were doubtful about coming out to teachers, recommended probably disclosing to counselors, and were most likely to suggest disclosing to friends. Females were even more reluctant than males to recommend disclosing their sexual orientation to the principal.

TABLE 4. Advice About Disclosure to Others

Disclose to:	Males		Females		t
	M^a	N	M	N	
Principal	3.05	85	3.39	84	2.53*
Teacher	2.54	85	2.73	90	1.30
Counselor	2.30	87	2.28	94	−.15
Friends	1.73	89	1.73	97	.01

a. 1 = yes; 2 = probably yes; 3 = probably no; 4 = no
*$p < .05$

Best and Worst Things About Disclosure

Best things. A number of males (N = 35) and females (N = 33) described the "best thing that ever happened to you" because of disclosing one's homosexuality to someone at school. Responses were very personal and difficult to categorize but were put into three categories which were not mutually exclusive and one category of "Other." The first category, Self Acceptance, included statements about feelings of increased self worth, relief, and the ability to be oneself. Examples of such responses are "reassurance that it's okay to be gay," "feel better," "gained confidence," and "I felt like a pressure was lifted." The category of Support and Friendship included statements such as "I received a very long supportive letter from someone I had originally thought would not respond well," "we became better friends," "gained new friends," and "life-long friendship developed."

The category of Sexual Relationships included explicit and implicit suggestions that coming out of the closet led to a sexual or romantic relationship, ranging from "I had a friend to whom I was attracted. We both played sports and spent a lot of time together. After we discussed my feelings he said he felt the same way. We have been together 10 years now" to "got laid" to "we had a relationship 12th grade into college." Somewhat overlapping with this category is the one of meeting other gay individuals and/or finding a gay support network, e.g., "Disclosure with friends who also happened to be gay provided support and a network" and "got to go to my first bar and meet people like me." Finally the Other category included miscellaneous comments from "Nothing–I just felt normal doing it" to "The reaction was so indifferent that it made no difference either positively or negatively."

Worst things. Twenty-three women and 26 men described "the worst thing that happened" because of disclosing one's homosexuality at school. These responses tended to fall into four categories, the first three of which were not mutually exclusive. First, some people reported negative effects on their interpersonal relationships, leading to losses of friendships or rejection from others. Examples include "when in college told a very close female friend. We are no longer friends because she doesn't believe in it," "I lost my best friend of 13 years," and "rejection-betrayal."

A second category reflected direct harassment and discrimination. Examples ranged from "name calling" and "teasing" to "somebody called me a fag, threatened to beat me up" to "got the shit kicked out of me." The third (and least common) category involved feelings of dishonesty and discomfort, exemplified by "I guess having to live with a certain amount of dishonesty to my friends, family, and myself" or "Could not be myself–I had to pretend to be someone I wasn't. Always lying." Contrary to the intent of the question, these responses seemed to reflect reactions to concealment rather than to disclosure. Finally, seven gay men and one lesbian explicitly stated that they experienced no negative consequences of disclosing their sexual orientation in school.

DISCUSSION

The findings of the present study are consistent with those of others who have suggested that schools can be a site for various manifestations of homophobia. This homophobia is intertwined with issues relating to gender and gender roles, and both males and females suffer from its effects. Although many participants in our study reported individual positive experiences as gay persons in the school system, almost all of them found various aspects of the school setting to be frightening, oppressive, and even dangerous. Before considering the implications of the results for individuals and schools, we would like to discuss issues related to the methodology of the study and to gender.

Methodological Issues

There are two methodological issues which may affect the interpretation of the findings of this study. First is the nature of the sample. Although participants came from a wide variety of occupations and from all over the country, the majority were well educated professional people from the Northeast. The wide range of ages meant that many of the participants went to school at a time in which prejudice against homosexuality and an unwillingness to discuss it may have been even more widespread than it is today. However, even recent articles indicate that schools remain centers of conservativism and anti-gay remarks (Casper, Schultz, & Wickens, 1992; Crumpacker & Vander Haegen 1987; Elia, 1993/94; Kielwasser & Wolf, 1993/94; Telljohann & Price, 1993; Uribe & Harbeck, 1991). Thus, even though the respondents' experiences as students occurred some time in their past, these experiences are probably still relevant today.

The second methodological issue is the nature of the measures. Unlike those studies which used detailed interviews with smaller samples (e.g., Casper et al., 1992; Sears, 1991; Uribe & Harbeck, 1991), we elected to preserve the anonymity of our participants by using a questionnaire format. The instrument contained a mixture of structured and open-ended questions to provide an opportunity for both quantitative and qualitative analyses. A substantial number of the respondents chose to answer all the questions. Although self report data are always subject to the possibility of bias, it is our impression, from examining the thoughtful written comments, that the participants were responding honestly and seriously.

Gender

Relatively few statistically significant gender differences in disclosure and in the reactions to disclosure were found. The males in our study had suspected they were gay, known for certain that they were gay, and told their siblings and friends that they were gay at significantly younger ages than the females. On the other hand, proportionately more females than males came out to others while in high school, and females who came out in school did so almost a grade before males. Moreover, only a minority of females disclosed their sexual orientation to males, whereas a majority of males came out to both males and females. These findings held for disclosure both to teachers and to friends. This preference for disclosing to females suggests that the belief that males are more prejudiced against homosexuals, particularly male homosexuals (Elia, 1993/94; Eliason, 1995; Herek, 1988; Kite & Whitley, 1996; Whitley & Kite, 1995), may be shared by our respondents. Alternatively, females may be seen as more appropriate confidantes for highly personal issues than males.

Implications

Implications for individuals. To tell or not to tell? Our respondents had no simple answers. They recognized the problems with secrecy and the potential benefits of openness (Harbeck, 1993/94; Matsko, 1989/90), yet they were also well aware of the pain, distress, and possible loss of relationships that might result from disclosure. Youth who are wrestling with possible loss of support from family, teachers, and friends if they reveal their known or suspected homosexuality should not be automatically urged to do so if they are living in an atmosphere in which some of the "worst things" which could happen to them are bad indeed.

Although there are some undeniably bad outcomes reported by our respondents who came out in a school setting, there were also many "best things." Many participants reported substantial support and enduring friendships that resulted from their openness. Others indicated that feelings of relief, integrity, and personal satisfaction were overwhelming and highly satisfying. Still others reported that contact with others who were gay enriched their lives. These findings should be encouraging to those who are contemplating "coming out of the classroom closet" (Harbeck, 1991). It is also clear that failure to be open about one's sexual orientation can also have negative outcomes, such as diminished ability to be a supportive warm friend and role model (Newton & Risch, 1981). An important topic for future research would be to identify the factors which predict successful or unsuccessful experiences with disclosure, including characteristics of the individual, the school setting, and the others in that setting.

Our respondents were conflicted in the advice that they would give others about disclosing their homosexuality in the school setting. The participants in this study were all "out" enough to be vacationing in an area frequented by gays and lesbians and to acknowledge their homosexuality on an anonymous questionnaire. Yet they were not sure enough that the advantages of openness outweighed the disadvantages to universally recommend disclosure. One could argue that individuals should not have to face the conflict between integrity and openness on the one hand and possible serious losses of friendships, jobs, and relationships with family on the other. It is the responsibility of members of society to change the general culture and particularly the schools, in order to create an atmosphere in which establishing and acknowledging one's identity should be no more difficult in the realm of sexuality than it is in other realms.

Implications for schools. The responses of our participants are consistent with other studies reporting that schools are settings in which homophobia survives, if not flourishes. Sears (1991, p. 39), for example, found that 80% of prospective teachers he surveyed "harbored negative feelings toward lesbians and gay men." Even those staff members and students who feel sympathetic and/or supportive towards gay and lesbian students, parents, and fellow teachers may lack basic knowledge about homosexuality (Harris et al., 1995; Harris & Vanderhoof, 1995; Sears, 1991).

A number of our respondents made statements indicating that they did not realize that they were homosexual when they were in school. Some stated that they were not aware of their sexuality, some were not gay at the time, some never considered it, and some were simply unsure. These findings suggest that schools should provide comprehensive sexuality education, including information about sexual orientation for all students, not just those who indicate that they are homosexual. The other articles in this collection are among those (Anderson, 1994; Elia, 1993/94; O'Conor, 1993/94; Reynolds & Koski, 1993/94; Rofes, 1989; Telljohann & Price, 1993; Uribe & Harbeck, 1991) which have provided specific suggestions for ways in which schools might address the needs of gay and lesbian students. Although our data do not speak directly to this issue, we certainly endorse these recommendations and believe that the participants in this study would agree.

REFERENCES

Anderson, J. D. (1994). School climate for gay and lesbian students and staff members. *Phi Delta Kappan, 76(2),* 151-154.

Casper, V., Schultz, S., & Wickens, E. (1992). Breaking the silence: Lesbian and gay parents and the schools. *Teachers College Record, 94,* 113-140.

Crumpacker, L., & Vander Haegen, E. M. (1987). Pedagogy and prejudice: Strategies for confronting homophobia in the classroom. *Women's Studies Quarterly, 3/4,* 65-72.

Elia, J. P. (1993/94). Homophobia in the high school: A problem in need of a resolution. *The High School Journal, 77,* 177-185.

Eliason, M. J. (1995). Attitudes about lesbians and gay men: A review and implications for social service training. *Journal of Gay & Lesbian Social Services, 2,* 73-90.

Harbeck, K. M. (Ed.). (1991). Coming out of the classroom closet: Gay and lesbian students, teachers, and curricula. [Special issue]. *Journal of Homosexuality, 22(3/4).*

Harbeck, K. M. (1993/94). Invisible no more: Addressing the needs of gay, lesbian, and bisexual youth and their advocates. *The High School Journal, 77,* 169-176.

Harris, M. B., Nightengale, J., & Owen, N. (1995). Health care professionals' experience, knowledge, and attitudes concerning homosexuality. *Journal of Gay & Lesbian Social Services, 2,* 91-107.

Harris, M. B., & Vanderhoof, J. (1995). Attitudes towards gays and lesbians serving in the military. *Journal of Gay & Lesbian Social Services, 3,* 23-51.

Herek, G. M. (1988). Heterosexuals' attitudes toward lesbians and gay men: Correlates and gender differences. *Journal of Sex Research, 25(4),* 451-477.

Herek, G. M., & Capitano, J. P. (1996). "Some of my best friends": Intergroup contact, concealable stigma, and heterosexuals' attitudes toward gay men and lesbians. *Personality and Social Psychology Bulletin, 22,* 412-424.

Kielwasser, A. P., & Wolf, M. A. (1993/94). Silence, difference, and annihilation: Understanding the impact of mediated heterosexism on high school students. *The High School Journal, 77,* 58-79.

Kite, M. (1992). Individual differences in males' reactions to gay males and lesbians. *Journal of Applied Social Psychology, 17,* 1222-1239.

Kite, M. E., & Whitley, B. E., Jr. (1996). Sex differences in attitudes toward homosexual persons, behaviors, and civil rights: A meta-analysis. *Personality and Social Psychology Bulletin, 22,* 336-353.

Kurdek, L. A. (1988). Correlates of negative attitudes toward homosexuals in heterosexual college students. *Sex Roles, 18*(11/12), 727-738.

Martin, A. D., & Hetrick, E. S. (1988). The stigmatization of the gay and lesbian adolescent. *Journal of Homosexuality, 15,* 163-183.

Matsko, V. (1989/90). My closet door swings wide. *Empathy, 2,* 6-8.

Newton, D. E., & Risch, S. J. (1981). Homosexuality and education: A review of the issue. *The High School Journal, 65,* 191-202.

O'Conor, A. (1993/94). Who gets called queer in school? Lesbian, gay, and bisexual teenagers, homophobia and high school. *The High School Journal, 77,* 7-12.

Oliver, M. B., & Hyde, J. S. (1993). Gender differences in sexuality: A meta-analysis. *Psychological Bulletin, 114,* 29-51.

Oliver, M. B., & Hyde, J. S. (1995). Gender differences in attitudes toward homosexuality: A reply to Whitley and Kite. *Psychological Bulletin, 115,* 155-158.

Reynolds, A. L., & Koski, M. J. (1993/94). Lesbian, gay, and bisexual teens and the school counselor: Building alliances. *The High School Journal, 77,* 88-93.

Rofes, E. (1989). Opening up the classroom closet: Responding to the educational needs of gay and lesbian youth. *Harvard Educational Review, 59,* 444-453.

Sears, J. T. (1991). Educators, homosexuality, and homosexual students: Are personal feelings related to professional beliefs? *Journal of Homosexuality, 22,* 29-79.

Telljohann, S. K., & Price, J. H. (1993). A qualitative examination of adolescent homosexuals' life experiences: Ramifications for secondary school personnel. *Journal of Homosexuality, 26,* 41-56.

Uribe, V. (1993/94). Project 10: A school-based outreach to gay and lesbian youth. *The High School Journal, 77,* 108-112.

Uribe, V., & Harbeck, K. M. (1991). Addressing the needs of lesbian, gay and bisexual youth: The origins of Project 10 and school-based intervention. *Journal of Homosexuality, 22,* 9-28.

Whitley, B. E., & Kite, M. E. (1995). Sex differences in attitudes towards homosexuality: A comment on Oliver and Hyde (1993). *Psychological Bulletin, 117,* 146-154.

The Sound of Silence:
Public School Response to the Needs
of Gay and Lesbian Youth

Janet H. Fontaine

SUMMARY. In spite of professional association leadership, public schools have been reluctant to accept responsibility for protecting sexual minority students against acts of harassment and discrimination. Study results show attitudes of students and educators toward homosexual youth have changed little over the past ten years. It is proposed that active involvement of educators in the creation of safe and supportive environments for gay and lesbian students is no longer optional due to recent court decisions. Problem areas and suggestions for developing gay supportive school environments are provided. *[Article copies available for a fee from The Haworth Document Delivery Service: 1-800-342-9678. E-mail address: getinfo@haworth.com]*

Estimates (AFSC Gay/Lesbian Youth Program, 1991) are that as many as 9 students in every classroom of 30 are in some measure affected by homosexual issues (having a gay or lesbian parent, sibling, relative, or being gay oneself). Yet even with this substantial number, the code of silence in our nation's school systems

Janet H. Fontaine is Associate Professor, Department of Counseling, Indiana University of Pennsylvania, Indiana, PA 15705. E-mail: FONTAINE@grove.iup.edu

[Haworth co-indexing entry note]: "The Sound of Silence: Public School Response to the Needs of Gay and Lesbian Youth." Fontaine, Janet H. Co-published simultaneously in *Journal of Gay & Lesbian Social Services* (The Haworth Press, Inc.) Vol. 7, No. 4, 1997, pp. 101-109; and: *School Experiences of Gay and Lesbian Youth: The Invisible Minority* (ed: Mary B. Harris) The Haworth Press, Inc., 1997, pp. 101-109; and: *School Experiences of Gay and Lesbian Youth: The Invisible Minority* (ed: Mary B. Harris) The Harrington Park Press, an imprint of The Haworth Press, Inc., 1997, pp. 101-109. Single or multiple copies of this article are available for a fee from The Haworth Document Delivery Service [1-800-342-9678, 9:00 a.m. - 5:00 p.m. (EST). E-mail address: getinfo@haworth.com].

concerning homosexuality remains. Breaking this code is essential to the physical and mental well being of our gay and lesbian youth. Supposedly committed to fostering national democratic traditions of justice for all, school systems often succumb to broader community pressure and fear of controversy. These motivations become more plausible and vivid with a review of several comments taken from a study surveying school counselors' experiences with gay and lesbian students (Fontaine, in press). Several counselors chose to add comments that reflected the extent of their frustrations with their school systems and administrators in not being more responsive to the needs of gay and lesbian youth.

> . . . the social stigma attached to the subject is very strong . . . Administrators run for cover when the subject is brought up, as it illicits (sic) too much controversy. School counselors are attacked by religious fundamentalist groups for appearing to *tolerate* homosexuality when we promote guidance topics such as respecting differences . . .

> The school community is probably the biggest road block. The head of the PTA won't allow stories of families with homosexual parents read in the class. They feel it is wrong and we should teach that it is wrong . . .

> I am concerned that Congress has threatened to cut off federal funding to school districts that teach alternative lifestyles. As a counselor, where does that leave me?

Reviewing these comments, it becomes glaringly apparent that there is a confluence of factors that influence the direction of efforts toward making schools and curricula more inclusive. Whether through indifference, homophobia, or efforts to avoid controversy, schools have taken the easier road and dismally failed to acknowledge the existence of and provide services for their gay and lesbian adolescent constituents.

Schools have failed to such an extent that the National Education Association (NEA) developed and adopted a resolution in 1988 specifically on student sexual orientation that proclaimed "all persons, regardless of sexual orientation, should be afforded equal opportunity within the public education system" (NEA, 1991, p. 19).

The cost of the abusive treatment homosexual youth receive in school and in the community is evident in terms of the documented human suffering they experience. This cost places gay and lesbian students at higher risk of school failure, suicide, depression, poor self-esteem, substance abuse, physical victimization, sexually transmitted diseases, and poor academic achievement than their heterosexual counterparts (Remafedi, 1987). These are students who are forced to learn in an environment where the norm is to ridicule and exclude anyone who is not perceived to be heterosexual.

They have endured in silence because little recourse within the system was available to them. This, however, may no longer be the case as more students may look to the nation's legal system for support to ensure their rights for equitable treatment under the Fourteenth Amendment are protected. Educators may no longer have the luxury of neglecting the needs of gay and lesbian youth in their schools.

The problem of silence regarding the status of gay and lesbian youth in our schools can be viewed as twofold–educational acts of omission and behavioral acts of commission.

THE EDUCATIONAL PROBLEM

Curriculum

The topic of homosexuality in educational curricula is almost nonexistent. Currently, gay or lesbian students find little in any course that even *validates* the existence of others like themselves. Examining existing course content would lead most gay and lesbian students to the conclusion that homosexuals have never existed nor contributed in any significant manner to our nation's history. Fontaine (in press) found only 14% of responding counselors indicated any inclusion of the topic of homosexuality in any courses in their schools.

In 1988, the National Education Association (1991) formally recognized that homosexual students experienced much greater "hostility and neglect" in school environments. Their subsequent *Training Handbook for Educators* (NEA, 1991) included a Bill of Rights for

Lesbian and Gay School Age Children that identified the right of every student to "have access to accurate information about themselves, free of negative judgment, and delivered by trained adults who not only inform them, but affirm them" (NEA, 1991, p. 40).

Teachers were encouraged by the NEA (1991) to include the contributions of homosexuals throughout the curriculum. While acknowledging that some courses (health, sex education, psychology) lend themselves more easily to discussions of homosexual issues, teachers of other subjects (language arts, American history, and government) were encouraged to explore the historical contributions of homosexuals and recognize role models in their disciplines. Helpful suggestions for educators to redesign courses to be more inclusive are plentiful (Besner & Spungin, 1995; NEA, 1991).

The open acknowledgement of homosexuality and homosexual persons in course content can begin to demythologize the topic. Prejudice and stereotypes diminish as understanding increases through educational efforts that provide accurate information. Developing inclusive course materials can assist in creating an atmosphere within the school that legitimizes, facilitates, and promotes the discussion of the topic and creates an environment that is more tolerant. For students struggling to come to grips with a socially stigmatized sexual identity, the inclusion of such information can lend hope and relief by providing role models, i.e., evidence that others before them have survived and become contributing members to society. At a point in their identity development when gay and lesbian adolescents are struggling to integrate a negatively stigmatized sexual identity, providing such information could be invaluable to the formation of a more positive self-concept.

Educational Resources

Resource materials for both faculty and students to learn more about homosexuality are nonexistent in most school libraries and media centers, further isolating the educational community and gay youth from information that could lend understanding and comfort. Besner and Spungin (1995) suggest media specialists have books, pamphlets, videos, and other materials available for both teachers and students. In addition, they suggest displaying materials in prominent places along with such advocacy activities as creating displays to highlight events such as Gay Pride Week.

THE BEHAVIORAL PROBLEM

A Question of Attitude

Students perceive teacher attitudes and feelings through the teacher's verbal and nonverbal behavior. Teacher attitudes can provide the validation for a gay student's self-acceptance or self-rejection. While educators are thus uniquely poised to play a primary role in the lives of adolescents because of their availability and daily contact, evidence indicates that their use of this role has been less than positive for sexual minority students. Telljohann and Price (1993) found only 20% of gay and lesbian students able to identify someone in their school who had been supportive to them. Sears (1992) reported 8 of 10 pre-service teachers harbored negative feelings and attitudes toward gays and lesbians while nearly two-thirds of school counselors in his study expressed similar feelings about homosexuality and homosexual persons.

Fontaine (in press) surveyed school counselors to determine current attitudes of students, faculty, and administrators toward homosexual students in their schools. Results reflected more intolerant attitudes toward gay and lesbian students than supportive ones. Using a 5-point scale (1 = intolerant; 5 = supportive), administrators were seen as the least intolerant (M = 2.74) with students being the most intolerant (M = 2.08). This latter finding, i.e., that students harbor the greatest degree of intolerance toward fellow gay and lesbian students, is supported by previous research and the many stories of abuse told by gay youth themselves (Harbeck, 1992; Nabozny, 1996; Remafedi, 1987).

Since media images and the popular press in the recent past have provided more positive images of gays and lesbians, it is conceivable that progress toward more tolerant attitudes has taken place. Unfortunately, evidence does not seem to support this view (Fontaine, in press). Perceived attitude changes of students, faculty, and administrators over the past 10 years were assessed using a 5-point scale (1 = less tolerant, 3 = no change, 5 = more tolerant). Mean ratings reflected little to no change in any of the groups (student M = 3.13; faculty M = 3.19; administrator M = 3.24). It would appear, based on these data, that even with this increased media visibility when combined with the efforts of professional organizations that encourage their memberships to become more tolerant and inclusive (National Association of School Psychologists, National Education Association, American School Health Association), little change has been effected in the daily implementation of educational programming and in individual educators' attitudes.

The hostility and intractability of these attitudes is even more apparent through comments of two school counselors taken from a recent study (Fontaine, in press).

> Gay/lesbian (sic) turn me off based on my own beliefs/prejudices. I find this morally reprehensible yet as a counselor I *am* morally bound to help such a student. If a youngster approaches me, only then will I do what I must do, to inform myself, not be judgmental, and to offer appropriate counseling.

> I believe that our society tends to take the illness in society and accept that illness rather then (sic) try to cure the illness. Please do not take me wrong. I hate the sin but I love the person. I just feel that if a person is ill, one trys (sic) to cure the illness not accept it and even promote it in society by telling the person the act and life style is 'ok.'

Direct approaches to changing attitudes toward homosexuals through educational programming have proven more successful (Rudolph, 1989). The *Training Handbook for Educators,* "Affording Equal Opportunity to Gay and Lesbian Students Through Teaching and Counseling," is the NEA's (1991) recognition of such and acknowledgement that attitude change is crucial to the creation of safe and supportive school environments. In the *Handbook,* school districts are encouraged to provide training for staff, school board members, parents, and other community-based groups in order to facilitate a better understanding of the problems that gay and lesbian youth face.

Inappropriate Behavior

The problem of verbal and physical abuse of gay and lesbian students in their schools is one of significant proportions. In one study, forty-five percent of gay males and 20% of lesbians experienced physical or verbal assault in high school. Twenty-eight percent of these students felt forced to drop out of school because of harassment based on their sexual orientation (Remafedi, 1987). Fontaine (in press) reported that 59% of responding counselors had actually observed 62 separate incidents of student harassment of gay and lesbian students that took the form of name-calling, teasing, ridicule, pushing, hitting, and shoving. One counselor noted that he knew of one male student who had quit school because of continuous homophobic comments made to him.

Such inappropriate behaviors can more easily be regulated than attitudes, and schools have the responsibility to do so. School regulations and policies are the most common means of addressing discriminatory behaviors (physical abuse, slurs, name-calling, etc.). Active enforcement of such policies is also necessary.

School anti-discrimination policies already exist in a number of schools. However, many such policies are designed to address racial discrimination and infrequently extend such protection to sexual minorities. Fontaine (in press) found 61% of surveyed counselors indicated a racial discrimination policy existed at their school yet only 39% of these (or approximately 24% of all school counselors surveyed), indicated that the policy included protection for homosexual students.

Inclusive school policies need to be established that foster the norm that the dignity and rights of all students will be respected in each school. Schools that do not actively provide for the protection of minority group members lend implicit support to the continued harassment of their marginal status. The National Education Association (1991) recommends school districts establish policies that recognize the rights of all students to:

- attend school free of verbal and physical harassment
- attend schools where respect and dignity for all is standard
- be included in all support programs that exist to help teenagers deal with the difficulties of adolescence

- attend schools where education, not survival, is the priority
- have a heritage free of crippling self-hate and unchallenged discrimination.

NO LONGER A MATTER OF CHOICE

The *voluntary compliance* of implementing an inclusive curriculum and providing a supportive environment for homosexual students may be a luxury of the past. Much like the civil rights movement of the 1960s, it appears the cause for equal rights for gay and lesbian students in public schools is turning to the nation's legal system to expedite its quest. A recent Wisconsin case may serve as the benchmark for what, undoubtedly, will sensitize school boards, administrators, and educators across the country to their responsibility to protect all youth in their schools, not just the heterosexual ones. In the case of Nabozny vs. several Ashland Public School District administrators (1996), the plaintiff, Jamie Nabozny, a homosexual, was awarded $1 million in damages for the treatment he endured while a student in the Ashland public school system. The suit cited continuing instances of physical abuse and verbal harassment for which school administrators took no action and were thus found liable for violating Nabozny's rights under the Fourteenth Amendment.

CONCLUSION

Due to the lack of healthy role models, support systems, and affirmation of who they are within their school system, gay and lesbian youth have little basis for developing feelings of self worth and positive aspirations for their future. Only in rare cases, where school personnel have been committed to the fair treatment and growth of all adolescents, are sexual minority youth supported by affirming policies. When educators fail to challenge homophobic remarks and establish and enforce anti-discrimination policies inclusive of sexual minority youth, they collude in the emotional and physical abuse of every adolescent in the school. The social norm of discrimination, exclusion, and abuse of certain classes of students is condoned.

The Nabozny case may serve as impetus for school districts to more actively support the rights of sexual minority youth or risk litigation. Comments cited here, however, indicate that successful implementation of such changes will take more than the mere creation of policy. Homophobic attitudes of all constituents will need to be addressed through training programs.

REFERENCES

AFSC Gay/Lesbian Youth Program. (1991). *Anti-bias training on gay/lesbian/bisexual youth.* Seattle, WA: Author.

Alyson, S. (Ed.). (1991). *Young, gay & proud.* Boston, MA: Alyson Publications, Inc.

Besner, H.F., & Spungin, C.J. (1995). *Gay & lesbian students: Understanding their needs.* Washington, DC: Taylor & Frances.

Fontaine, J.H. (in press). Evidencing a need: School counselors' experience with gay and lesbian students. *The School Counselor.*

Fricke, A. (1981). *Reflections of a rock lobster: A story about growing up gay.* Boston, MA: Alyson Publications.

Harbeck, K.M. (Ed.). (1992). *Coming out of the classroom closet: Gay and lesbian students, teachers and curricula.* New York: The Harrington Park Press.

Heron, A. (Ed.). (1983). *One teenager in ten.* Boston: Alyson Publications.

Nabozny v. Podlesny, Davis, Blauert et al., No. 95-C-086 (7th Cir. July 31, 1996).

National Education Association. (1991). *Affording equal opportunity to gay and lesbian students through teaching and counseling: A training handbook for educators.* Washington, DC: Author.

Remafedi, G. (1987). Adolescent homosexuality: Psychosocial and medical implications. *Pediatrics, 79*(3), 331-337.

Rudolph, J. (1989). Effects of a workshop on mental health practitioners' attitudes toward homosexuality and counseling effectiveness. *Journal of Counseling & Development, 68,* 81-85.

Sears, J.T. (1992). Educators, homosexuality, and homosexual students: Are personal feelings related to professional beliefs? In K.M. Harbeck (Ed.), *Coming out of the classroom closet: Gay and lesbian students, teachers, and curricula* (pp. 29-79). Binghamton, NY: The Harrington Park Press.

Telljohann, S., & Price, J. (1993). A qualitative examination of adolescent homosexuals' life experiences: Ramifications for secondary school personnel. *Journal of Homosexuality, 26*(1), 41-56.

Index

Administrators
  liability of, xvi
  role of, 12,108
Adolescence
  defined, 2
  outcome expectations and, 4
  self-efficacy beliefs and, 4
Affirmative environments, 11
Alcohol abuse, 29
Alienation, 44-45
American Psychological Association
  Policy Statement on
  Lesbian and Gay Issues, 80
Anti-gay attacks, 67
Anti-gay victimization, 68-69
Anxiety
  disclosure of sexual orientation
   and, 27-29
  measures of, 23
  negative feelings and, 28-29
ATLG. *See* Attitudes Toward
  Lesbians and Gay Men
  (ATLG)
Attitudes Toward Lesbians and Gay
  Men (ATLG), 72,78

Bandura, A., 3-4
Bias crimes, 66
Bill of Rights for Lesbian and Gay
  School Age Children,
  103-104
Bisexual adolescents (female/male)
  career development of, 7-8
  coming out and, 97
  as gifted children, 21
  identity in schools and, 53-54

middle school years of, 54-55
  peer groups and, 54-55
  school climates and, 18,79
Bliss, G. K., 85-99
Brown, S. D., 3-4

Career development
  environmental variables of, 7
  integrating sexual orientation and, 9
  lack of role models and, 8
  of lesbian, gay, and bisexual
   adolescents, 7-8
  lesbian/gay adolescents and, 1-12
  minority-group models of, 7
  women and, 7
Career theories, 3
Charter schools, xiv
Circumscription and compromise,
  theory of, 7
Coming out. *See also* Disclosure, of
  sexual orientation
  negative experiences, 27,29-30
  positive experiences, 25-26,29
Counselors
  need for support of, 43
  reluctance to intervene of, 5-6
Curriculum
  homosexual issues and, 103-104
  mandatory inclusive, 108
  supporting heterosexism, 57-58

DBS. *See* Discriminatory Behaviors
  Scale (DBS)
Depression, 46-47
Derogatory language. *See* Verbal
  harassment

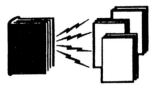

Haworth
DOCUMENT DELIVERY
SERVICE

This valuable service provides a single-article order form for any article from a Haworth journal.

- *Time Saving:* No running around from library to library to find a specific article.
- *Cost Effective:* All costs are kept down to a minimum.
- *Fast Delivery:* Choose from several options, including same-day FAX.
- *No Copyright Hassles:* You will be supplied by the original publisher.
- *Easy Payment:* Choose from several easy payment methods.

Open Accounts Welcome for ...
- Library Interlibrary Loan Departments
- Library Network/Consortia Wishing to Provide Single-Article Services
- Indexing/Abstracting Services with Single Article Provision Services
- Document Provision Brokers and Freelance Information Service Providers

---

MAIL or *FAX* THIS ENTIRE ORDER FORM TO:

Haworth Document Delivery Service
The Haworth Press, Inc.
10 Alice Street
Binghamton, NY 13904-1580

or FAX: 1-800-895-0582
or CALL: 1-800-342-9678
9am-5pm EST

PLEASE SEND ME PHOTOCOPIES OF THE FOLLOWING SINGLE ARTICLES:

1) Journal Title: _____

   Vol/Issue/Year: _____ Starting & Ending Pages: _____

   Article Title: _____

   _____

2) Journal Title: _____

   Vol/Issue/Year: _____ Starting & Ending Pages: _____

   Article Title: _____

   _____

3) Journal Title: _____

   Vol/Issue/Year: _____ Starting & Ending Pages: _____

   Article Title: _____

   _____

4) Journal Title: _____

   Vol/Issue/Year: _____ Starting & Ending Pages: _____

   Article Title: _____

   _____

(See other side for Costs and Payment Information)

COSTS: Please figure your cost to order quality copies of an article.

1. Set-up charge per article: $8.00
   ($8.00 × number of separate articles)   _____
2. Photocopying charge for each article:

   1-10 pages: $1.00   _____

   11-19 pages: $3.00   _____

   20-29 pages: $5.00   _____

   30+ pages: $2.00/10 pages   _____

3. Flexicover (optional): $2.00/article   _____
4. Postage & Handling: US: $1.00 for the first article/

   $.50 each additional article   _____

   Federal Express: $25.00   _____

   Outside US: $2.00 for first article/
   $.50 each additional article_____

5. Same-day FAX service: $.35 per page   _____

                              GRAND TOTAL: _____

METHOD OF PAYMENT: (please check one)

❑ Check enclosed   ❑ Please ship and bill. PO # _____
                    (sorry we can ship and bill to bookstores only! All others must pre-pay)

❑ Charge to my credit card: ❑ Visa; ❑ MasterCard; ❑ Discover;
                             ❑ American Express;

Account Number:_____ Expiration date:_____

Signature: **X**_____

Name: _____ Institution: _____

Address: _____

          _____

City: _____ State:_____ Zip:_____

Phone Number: _____ FAX Number: _____

MAIL or *FAX* THIS ENTIRE ORDER FORM TO:

Haworth Document Delivery Service	**or FAX:** 1-800-895-0582
The Haworth Press, Inc.	**or CALL:** 1-800-342-9678
10 Alice Street	9am-5pm EST)
Binghamton, NY 13904-1580	

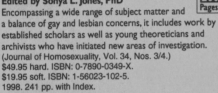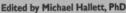 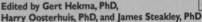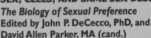

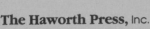